SEA FISHES
of Australia

T0342722

First published in 2024 by
Reed New Holland Publishers

Sydney

Level 1, 178 Fox Valley Road, Wahroonga,
NSW 2076, Australia

newhollandpublishers.com

A record of this book is held at the
National Library of Australia.

ISBN 9781760796310

Managing Director: Fiona Schultz
Publisher and Project Editor: Simon Papps
Designer: Andrew Davies
Production Director: Arlene Gippert

Printed in China

10 9 8 7 6 5 4 3 2 1

Keep up with Reed New Holland
and New Holland Publishers

f ReedNewHolland
@ @NewHollandPublishers
and @ReedNewHolland

Front cover: Harlequin Filefish.
Page 1: Pink Anemonefish.
Back cover: Orange Basslet.

Other titles in the Reed Concise Guides
series:

Animals of Australia
Ken Stepnell
ISBN 978 1 92151 754 9

Birds of Australia
Ken Stepnell
ISBN 978 1 92151 753 2

Butterflies of Australia
Paul Zborowski
ISBN 978 1 92554 694 1

Ferns of Australia
David L Jones
ISBN 978 1 76079 634 1

Frogs of Australia
Marion Anstis
ISBN 978 1 92151 790 7

Insects of Australia
Paul Zborowski
ISBN 978 1 92554 644 6

Lilies of Australia
David L Jones
ISBN 978 1 76079 617 4

Snakes of Australia
Gerry Swan
ISBN 978 1 92151 789 1

Spiders of Australia
Volker W Framenau and Melissa L Thomas
ISBN 978 1 92554 603 3

Trees of Australia
David L Jones
ISBN 978 1 92554 688 0

Wild Flowers of Australia
Ken Stepnell
ISBN 978 1 92151 755 6

For details of these books and hundreds
of other Natural History titles see
newhollandpublishers.com

CONTENTS

Fish Families and Species

4

5

Australia is home to numerous angelfish, including the rare Conspicuous Angelfish.

INTRODUCTION

The seas around Australia are filled with some of the world's most diverse and fascinating sea fishes. More than 4,000 marine fishes are found in Australian waters, with more being discovered each year, and these are grouped into over 200 families based on similar characteristics.

Australia is the largest island in the world, with the country's vast coastline blessed with a huge variety of habitats for marine fishes. In the north, Australia's warm tropical waters are filled with colourful reef fishes. Most of these tropical fishes are shared with other Indo-Pacific nations. While in the south, the nation's cool temperate waters are populated with mostly endemic fishes – species seen nowhere else on the planet.

Sea fishes are found in large numbers in every marine environment around Australia – mangroves, coral reefs, kelp forests, sandy bays and estuaries, and in the deep dark waters off the continental shelf. Some also play an important role in the seafood industry.

This concise guide features 121 families and 193 species – just a fraction of the species seen in Australia, but a great introduction to the wonderful variety of sea fishes found Down Under.

Abbreviations used in the text:

c.	circa, approximately
NSW	New South Wales
NT	Northern Territory
Qld	Queensland
SA	South Australia
Tas	Tasmania
Vic	Victoria
WA	Western Australia

SPECIES IN THIS BOOK

This concise guide is a great introduction to these fascinating marine creatures. The fish families presented in this book are the most common and the most interesting ones encountered by divers, snorkelers and anglers.

For each family, details are given about characteristics, number of species and any normal or interesting behaviour. The figure mentioned in brackets after the family header is the number of species from that family found in waters around Australia.

For many families, only one typical species has been selected to represent the group, with its picture and information about its size, description, habitat, range (given clockwise around the country) and any comments. The measurement at the start of each species account is the length of an average adult of that species, unless otherwise stated. In families with a diverse variety of species, more than one fish is included to illustrate these variations.

This guide also includes additional information about different habitats, fish biology and behaviour, dangerous fishes, responsible fishing practises and the weird and very complex reproductive strategies of fishes.

HABITATS

Australia is a very large country, with more than 70,000km of coastline, and around the nation are a great variety of marine habitats. While the coral reefs of the Great Barrier Reef contain the greatest number of fish species, fishes inhabit all marine ecosystems around the country.

Mangroves and estuaries are very important to many fish species, as some live permanently in this habitat, while others use it as a nursery for their young. A surprising number of fish live on, in and around the sand. This deceptively barren-looking habitat provides food and a place to hide for many species.

Coral reefs have a variety of habitats, as fishes can be found

The Shorthead Seahorse's preferred habitat is seagrasses.

in sheltered lagoons, on reef flats, in calm coral gardens or along reef walls washed by currents. Some fish like calm water, while others favour areas with currents, as these running waters bring them food.

In cooler temperate waters fish inhabit rocky reefs in deep and shallow water and sheltered bays with seagrasses, algae and kelp. The rocky reefs of southern Australia are known collectively as the Great Southern Reef and it is equally as important as the Great Barrier Reef for fishes. Most fishes found in cooler temperate environments are endemic and unique, with many fish families found nowhere else on Earth.

Most fish live in either tropical or temperate zones. However, between these zones is the subtropical region, which is a mixing ground of fishes from both regions, and it also hosts a few of its own unique fish species.

BIOLOGY

The first fishes evolved more than 500 million years ago. They were the first vertebrates and they are still the most diverse and complex group of vertebrate animals on the planet.

There are three main classes of fishes – jawless fishes, cartilaginous fishes and bony fishes. They all evolved on separate evolutionary lines, but share similar basic characteristics. All fish have fins for movement, gills for breathing, a supporting skeleton, a dorsal hollow nerve cord and a tail. However, they vary so much in shape and size that they have been split into classes, subclasses and families that group species together with similar characteristics.

The cartilaginous fishes, class Chondrichthyes, contains the sharks, rays and chimaeras (not included in this book). The sharks and rays are grouped in the subclass Elasmobranchii or strap-gilled fishes, as these animals have five to seven gill slits. These fishes also have a skeleton made of cartilage, practise internal fertilisation, and either lay eggs or give birth to live young.

The bony fishes, class Osteichthyes, are split into two subclasses. The Sarcopterygii are primitive fleshy finned fishes, with the best-known example being the Australian Lungfish,

The Australian Lungfish is a primitive fleshy finned freshwater fish.

although this is only found in freshwater so not included in this book. The more complex Actinopterygii subclass contains all the well-known ray-finned fishes, which make up 95 per cent of all known fishes. These fishes have a bony skeleton, fins supported by rays of dermal bone and a single gill opening on each side of the head. The bony fishes mainly reproduce with external fertilisation, which varies considerably.

The jawless fishes, class Agnatha, are primitive fishes with no real jaw. They are not included in this guide as they are rarely encountered.

BEHAVIOUR

The fishes are a very complex group of animals that display a very diverse range of behaviours. Bottom-dwelling fish live on the

The Footballer Sweep is a typical ray-finned fish species.

seafloor. These fish sit on the bottom, live in holes or under ledges, hide in the sand or swim close to the bottom. Mid-water fish swim in the water column and either feed in mid-water or on the seafloor. Most mid-water fish return to the bottom to avoid predators and sleep. Pelagic fish live in mid-water or near the surface, often in the open ocean, and some never visit the seafloor at any stage of their life.

Fish feed on a variety of foods in a variety of different ways. Some fish eat seaweeds and algae, but the great majority are carnivores. They consume sponges, corals, crustaceans, molluscs, echinoderms, worms, other fish, marine reptiles and marine mammals. Some small fish, and the biggest of all the fish, the Whale Shark, consume tiny plankton.

Many bottom-dwelling fish use camouflage, like this Glauert's Frogfish.

Some fish are territorial and have a very limited range, while others roam far and wide. Other fish are secretive and cryptic, using camouflage to conceal themselves from predators, while others use camouflage to ambush prey. A few fish live in symbiotic relationships with other animals, including many that clean other fishes, while others are almost parasitic, attaching themselves to larger fish and animals.

Fish are not simple animals that feel no pain. They have a central nervous system and keen senses. In some fish eyesight is very important, while in other fish their hearing is exceptional. However, in many fish their sense of smell is critical for finding food. Fish not only have the same five senses that all animals have, but also posses a sixth, call the lateral line, that detects pressure differences and water movement. Some fish can also detect electrical signals made by other animals, and a few can also generate their own electric shocks for defence.

Fish are also quite intelligent and have good memories. Sharks have been shown to be as intelligent as dogs, while most fish are quick to learn from their mistakes, to help them survive. Anyone that has dived or snorkelled with fish quickly discovers that these animals have very different personalities – some are friendly, some are shy, some are curious and others are very bossy.

We still know very little about the lives of most fishes, but what has been learnt is fascinating.

REPRODUCTION

Fish have the most interesting and fascinating sex lives of any animal group. Most sharks and rays have a simple reproductive strategy, as they mate like mammals, and then either lay eggs or give birth to live young. However, Grey Nurse Shark babies eat their siblings while in-utero, and several captive sharks and rays have got pregnant without ever mating and produced clones of themselves!

The bony fishes are even more bizarre, as many can change sex. In the wrasse family the male is the boss and has a harem of females. If he dies the largest female changes sex and takes his place. Anemonefish are the opposite, with a dominant female ruling the anemone. When she dies her male partner changes sex and takes her place. Other fish are born as females and can change sex to male as they age, while some can switch back and forth.

Most bony fishes spawn, with the male and female releasing

Male Pink Anemonefish tending eggs.

sperm and eggs. Some release them straight into the water column to drift away with the currents, while others attach the eggs to the bottom. Some guard their eggs, others don't. Some fish attach their eggs to themselves to keep them safe, and some keep their eggs in their mouth and are known as mouth brooders.

However, the seahorses have really switched things up in the mating world, with the male getting pregnant. Male seahorses have a stomach pouch where they keep the fertilised eggs until they hatch.

The sex lives of fish would make for a very interesting soap opera.

DANGEROUS FISHES

Ask any Australian and they would say that sharks are the most dangerous fish in the sea. However, most sharks pose little threat to people and there are many more potentially dangerous fish in the sea.

Numerous fish are venomous, with spines filled with toxins. The most dangerous are the scorpionfishes and stonefishes, which have fins brimming with toxins. These fish should never be touched or handled, and care should be taken when walking in shallow water where these fish hide. Additional venomous fishes include the catfishes, rabbitfishes and rays.

Other fishes are poisonous and should never be eaten. These poisons can be in the flesh or skin in species like pufferfishes, porcupinefishes, moray eels and boxfishes. Some tropical fish carry ciguatera in their flesh from eating algae, including triggerfishes, surgeonfishes and gropers.

Other fish have sharp teeth or spines, and should never be touched or harassed, these include the moray eels, flatheads, leatherjackets and surgeonfishes. Some fish are territorial in the breeding season and bite divers and snorkellers, so keep an eye out for angry damselfishes and triggerfishes.

Most sharks are small, shy and wary of people. In fact, the great majority of sharks are completely harmless. However, there are a few potentially dangerous sharks in Australian waters that have bitten people and resulted in fatalities. The risk of shark attack is very low, but you can reduce this risk even more by never swimming alone, especially on isolated beaches, never swim in murky water, never swim in schools of fish and stick to patrolled beaches and between the flags.

The Estuary Stonefish is a highly venomous fish that buries in the sand.

Most fishes are not aggressive and pose no real threat if treated with respect.

RESPONSIBLE FISHING

Fishing is a popular activity in Australia and it should always be done in a responsible way. Ensure you know your fishes, know the size and catch limit, and the species that are protected.

Don't fish in marine reserves as they are there to ensure fish populations have a chance to breed and maintain numbers. Research scientists have estimated that we need 30% of the marine environment protected to maintain healthy fish populations. Unfortunately, we have far less than this protected in Australia, so every marine reserve is vital.

Fish feel pain, so remove hooks quickly and return undersized fish as fast as possible to the ocean. Fish you are keeping should be killed quickly and humanely. If spearfishing, only target the fish you are going to eat.

Always use biodegradable fish hooks. If you can't remove the hook, cut the line as close as possible to the hook. Also dispose of unwanted fishing line responsibly.

Australian sea fishes play an important role in maintaining a healthy marine environment, and are a key link in the food chain that can be broken or stressed when overfished.

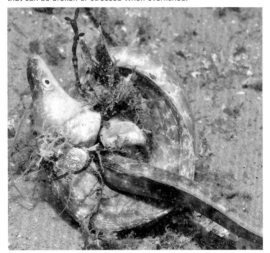

Moray eels often take anglers bait and some die from getting tangled in fishing line.

FISH FAMILIES
AND SPECIES

ANGELSHARKS (4 species)

Secretive flat-bodied sharks that hide under a layer of sand and ambush prey. Use their very sharp teeth to feed on fish, squid, octopus and crustaceans. They give birth to live young.

Australian Angelshark *Squatina australis*

ID: 152cm. Sandy or brown colour, with small white spots.

HABITAT/RANGE: Sandy bottoms from central NSW to southern WA.

NOTES: The most common angelshark in Australia, but very hard to find. Sometimes emerges at night and hunt for prey.

HORNSHARKS (3 species)

Primitive small shark species that still have horns in front of their dorsal fins. Mainly eat invertebrates, which are crushed by their tiny teeth, and they lay corkscrew-shaped eggs.

Port Jackson Hornshark
Heterodontus portusjacksoni

ID: 170cm. Sandy colour with a dark harness-like band pattern.

HABITAT/RANGE: Rocky reefs from northern NSW to central WA.

NOTES: Common in some areas. Best seen during winter when they gather in shallow water to breed.

MACKEREL SHARKS (3 species)

Large predatory sharks that roam open water in search of prey, feeding on everything from fish to marine mammals. They give birth to live young and most species are considered potentially dangerous.

Great White Shark *Carcharodon carcharias*

ID: 640cm. Dark grey to bronze dorsal surface and a white belly.

HABITAT/RANGE: Rocky reefs, offshore islands and open water from central Qld to central WA.

NOTES: The most infamous of all sharks and responsible for numerous attacks on humans. Fully protected in Australia.

SANDTIGER SHARKS (2 species)

Sandtiger sharks have long dagger-like teeth that make them look mean and aggressive. However, these teeth are designed to grip fish and not cut through flesh. They give birth to live young and have small litters, where the young are known to eat their siblings.

Grey Nurse Shark *Carcharias taurus*

ID: 320cm. Grey on the dorsal surface with a scattering of darker spots.

HABITAT/RANGE: Rocky reefs off central WA, southern Qld and NSW.

NOTES: Generally seen in packs by day, then spilt up at night to feed. Protected in Australia.

COLLARED CARPET SHARKS (5 species)

Small elongated sharks that hide under ledges or among seaweed by day, and hunt at night for small fish and crustaceans. They lay eggs and most live in deep water.

Varied Carpet Shark *Parascyllium variolatum*

ID: 92cm. Greyish body with darker bands and white spots, and a black collar with dense white spots.

HABITAT/RANGE: Rocky reefs covered in seaweed from Vic to southern WA.

NOTES: These nocturnal sharks are very secretive and rarely seen.

BLIND SHARKS (2 species)

Shy bottom-dwelling sharks only found off eastern Australia. These small sharks give birth to live young and feed at night on small fish and invertebrates.

Blind Shark *Brachaelurus waddi*

ID: 120cm. Brown with darker bands and a scattering of white spots.

HABITAT/RANGE: Rocky reefs off southern Qld and throughout NSW.

NOTES: A shy shark that hides under ledges by day to avoid being eaten by wobbegongs.

WOBBEGONGS (10 species)

An iconic Australian shark family, wobbegongs are renowned for their camouflaged skin pattern and shaggy 'beard'. These sharks are ambush predators with very sharp teeth that eat fish and invertebrates; they have also bitten numerous divers and spearfishers. They give birth to live young.

Spotted Wobbegong *Orectolobus maculatus*

ID: 170cm. Light to dark brown with paler ring-like markings.

HABITAT/RANGE: Rocky reefs from southern Qld to central WA, except Tas and parts of Vic.

NOTES: Although appearing lazy and sleepy, these sharks have quick reflexes and can grab a passing fish or a diver's hand.

BAMBOO SHARKS (3 species)

Small and slender bottom-dwellers that rest under ledges by day
and feed at night on fish and invertebrates. The family contains
two branches, with the bamboo sharks having plain colours and the
epaulette sharks having decorative patterns. These sharks lay eggs
and three species are found around Australia.

Greater Bamboo Shark *Chiloscyllium magnus*

ID: 140cm. Grey with faint bands.

HABITAT/RANGE: Coral and rocky reefs from northern WA to
northern NSW.

NOTES: A recently described species that is very common off
southern Qld, where groups are found sheltering under ledges.

Epaulette Shark *Hemiscyllium ocellatum*

ID: 107cm. Pale brown with small dark spots and a large epaulette spot near the gills.

HABITAT/RANGE: Coral reefs off Qld.

NOTES: Often found on reef flats, this shark can walk across the bottom, even on land, hence the nickname of 'walking shark'.

LEOPARD SHARK (1 species)

The only member of its family, the Leopard Shark is a very
distinctive shark with its long tail and ridges running along its body.
These sharks rest by day and feed at night on fish, crustaceans
and molluscs. They lay eggs and the young have a zebra-like skin
pattern, hence the alternative name of Zebra Shark.

Leopard Shark *Stegostoma tigrinum*

ID: 250cm. Light brown with leopard-like skin pattern.

HABITAT/RANGE: Coral and rocky reefs from northern WA to
northern NSW.

NOTES: These sharks migrate south over summer and are seen in
large numbers off southern Qld. A very docile shark.

NURSE SHARKS (1 species)

Only one member of this family is found in Australian waters – the Tawny Nurse Shark. This is a large reef shark with small teeth that eats fish and invertebrates it sucks into its mouth. These sharks give birth to live young.

Tawny Nurse Shark *Nebrius ferrugineus*

ID: 320cm. Grey- to brown-coloured shark.

HABITAT/RANGE: Coral and rocky reefs from northern WA to southern Qld.

NOTES: A nocturnal hunter, these sharks are generally seen sleeping in caves by day. They are quite docile but can be easily startled.

WHALE SHARK (1 species)

The largest fish in the world, the Whale Shark is the only member of its family. These immense sharks feed on plankton swallowed by their large broad mouth. Found in tropical and subtropical waters around the world and known to migrate vast distances. They give birth to live young.

Whale Shark *Rhincodon typus*

ID: 1200cm. Grey or brown with white spots.

HABITAT/RANGE: Open water from central WA to central NSW.

NOTES: Known to aggregate in large numbers at popular feeding spots, such as Ningaloo Reef off WA.

CATSHARKS (32 species)

A very large family of small bottom-dwelling sharks. Most species live in deep water and are never seen, but a few live in the shallows. These sharks have small teeth, feed on fish and invertebrates, and lay eggs.

Draughtboard Shark *Cephaloscyllium laticeps*

ID: 100cm. Greyish-brown with darker blotches and spots.

HABITAT/RANGE: Rocky reefs from southern NSW to southern WA, most common off Tas.

NOTES: This species can swell by ingesting water to deter predators such as seals and larger sharks.

WHALER SHARKS (30 species)

This family contains the classic-shaped sharks that most people are familiar with. These sharks all have large sharp teeth, and feed on a variety of prey, depending on the species, that includes fish, other sharks, rays, turtles and marine mammals. Several members are potentially dangerous, especially the Bull Shark (Carcharhinus leucas) and Tiger Shark. These sharks give birth to live young.

Tiger Shark *Galeocerdo cuvier*

ID: 550cm. Grey with faint bands and a blunt nose.

HABITAT/RANGE: Open water near reefs, from central WA to central NSW.

NOTES: A large and potentially dangerous shark that eats turtles and cleans up whale carcasses.

Whitetip Reef Shark *Triaenodon obesus*

ID: 213cm. Grey with white tips to the dorsal fins.

HABITAT/RANGE: Coral reefs from northern WA to southern Qld.

NOTES: Not considered dangerous, this species likes to rest in caves by day (unlike its cousins that must keep moving to breath) and hunts fish by night.

HAMMERHEAD SHARKS (4 species)

The most recently evolved family of sharks, with their hammer-shaped heads giving them a great advantage in detecting hidden prey. These sharks hunt fish, rays and cephalopods, and give birth to live young.

Scalloped Hammerhead *Sphyrna lewini*

ID: 350cm. Grey with a hammer-shaped head.

HABITAT/RANGE: Coral reefs from southern WA to central NSW.

NOTES: Often form into vast schools that migrate according to changes in sea temperature.

WEDGEFISHES (3 species)

Often mistaken for sharks, as they have a shark-like body and high dorsal fins. However, like all rays they have their pectoral fins fused with the head (in a wedge shape) and their gills on their ventral surface. These rays eat fish and invertebrates, which are mostly dug out of the sand. They give birth to live young.

Whitespotted Wedgefish *Rhynchobatus australiae*

ID: 300cm. Grey with white spots on the pectoral fins.

HABITAT/RANGE: Sandy bottoms from central WA to northern NSW.

NOTES: A rare species in most areas, however large numbers are found off southern Qld.

GIANT GUITARFISHES (1 species)

There are four families of rays with shovel-shaped heads, although only three of the families are featured in this guide. The giant guitarfishes are large sandy-coloured rays that are more closely related to sawfishes than other shovelnose rays. They eat small fish and invertebrates, and give birth to live young.

Giant Guitarfish *Glaucostegus typus*

ID: 270cm. A sand-coloured ray.

HABITAT/RANGE: Sandy bottoms from central WA to northern NSW.

NOTES: These rays like to bury in the sand and sometimes gather in groups in lagoons, with Heron Island a good place to see them.

BANJO RAYS (5 species)

Banjo rays are shovelnose rays that come in two forms – some have a shovel-shaped head and others have a rounded head. Members of this family also have patterned skin, with either stripes or blotches. Like most rays they feed on the bottom on small fish and invertebrates and give birth to live young.

Eastern Shovelnose Ray *Aptychotrema rostrata*

ID: 120cm. Sandy coloured with blotches.

HABITAT/RANGE: Sand or reefs off Qld and NSW.

NOTES: Generally bury in the sand by day and feed at night.

Southern Fiddler Ray *Trygonorrhina dumerilii*

ID: 146cm. Sandy coloured with a round head and darker stripes.

HABITAT/RANGE: Sand or reefs from Vic to southern WA.

NOTES: Often hidden under sand or kelp, there is a black-and-white form of this ray sometimes seen off South Australia.

COFFIN RAY (1 species)

The only member of its family, which is one of four families of electric rays. These rays generate electric shocks by rubbing modified muscles together. They use these shocks for self-defence and to stun prey. Coffin rays eat fish and invertebrates and give birth to live young.

Coffin Ray *Hypnos monopterygius*

ID: 63cm. Round shape and varies in colour from pale brown to dark brown.

HABITAT/RANGE: Sandy bottoms off Qld, NSW, SA and WA.

NOTES: Anyone zapped by one of these rays never forgets the experience. They hide under the sand and are very difficult to see.

SKATES (23 species)

Most skates live in deep water, so are rarely encountered by humans. However, a few species live in shallow water in temperate areas. These rays look superficially like a stingray, but have a short tail with small dorsal fins and they lack a defensive spine, instead having thorns on their back and tail. Skates are the only rays that lay eggs, and they feed on small fish and invertebrates.

Melbourne Skate *Spiniraja whitleyi*

ID: 200cm. Grey with small white spots.

HABITAT/RANGE: Sandy bottoms from southern NSW to southern WA.

NOTES: The largest Australian skate, this species rests on the sand near rocky reefs by day and feeds at night.

BUTTERFLY RAYS (1 species)

Very odd-looking rays with a lozenge-shaped disc that resembles a large taco. They also have a tiny tail and are very flat bodied, which helps them to hide under the sand. These rays give birth to live young and eat invertebrates and small fish.

Australian Butterfly Ray *Gymnura australis*

ID: 94cm wide. Sandy in colour with dark spots and lighter blotches.

HABITAT/RANGE: Sandy bottoms from central WA to central NSW.

NOTES: A rarely seen ray, but sometimes captured by trawlers.

STINGRAYS (25 species)

The stingray family is very diverse, displaying a range of sizes and body shapes. Most species have one or more dagger-like spines on their tail that can be regrown if lost. These spines are used for defence against predators such as sharks. The tails of stingrays vary greatly – some are long and whip-like, while others are short and some have skin folds. Stingrays are bottom feeders that prey on fish and invertebrates. They give birth to live young.

Smooth Stingray *Bathytoshia brevicaudata*

ID: 240cm wide. Black to grey with a V-shaped pattern of white spots across the disc.

HABITAT/RANGE: Rocky reefs from southern Qld to central WA.

NOTES: One of the largest stingrays in the world. Common in bays and under jetties, especially in areas where anglers clean their catch.

Australian Bluespotted Maskray
Neotrygon australiae

ID: 38cm wide. Pale brown with large blue spots.

HABITAT/RANGE: Sandy bottoms from central WA to central NSW.

NOTES: There are several bluespotted maskray species found throughout the Indo-Pacific that were once thought to be one species. The range of this species is still to be confirmed.

Porcupine Ray *Urogymnus asperrimus*

ID: 115cm wide. Greyish with thorns all over the disc and tail.

HABITAT/RANGE: Sandy bottoms from central WA to southern Qld.

NOTES: This round-shaped stingray is the only member of the family without a tail spine for defence.

STINGAREE (21 species)

Resemble a small stingray, with a short tail and tail spines for defence. Disc varies in shape from round to oval to rhomboidal. Mostly live in shallow water, often in groups, and feed on small fish and invertebrates. They give birth to live young.

Common Stingaree *Trygonoptera testacea*

ID: 25cm wide. Sandy colour with a small dorsal fin on a short tail.

HABITAT/RANGE: Sandy bottoms off southern Qld and throughout NSW.

NOTES: These little rays hide under the sand by day and can often be found in groups in shallow water.

EAGLE RAYS (4 species)

The eagle rays were recently split into two families, with the ones in this family having a rounded head and snout. Eagle rays feed on the bottom on small fish and invertebrates, but spend much of their time swimming around. Most of these rays have a tail spine and a long whip-like tail. They give birth to live young.

Southern Eagle Ray *Myliobatis tenuicaudatus*

ID: 160cm wide. Brown to olive with blue spots and bars.

HABITAT/RANGE: Temperate reefs from southern Qld to southern WA.

NOTES: Unlike other eagle rays, this species is often seen resting on the bottom and will cover itself in a layer of sand.

PELAGIC EAGLE RAYS (1 species)

These graceful rays come to the bottom to feed on fish and invertebrates, but spend most of their time swimming in mid-water. Pelagic eagle rays have a narrow head, a pointed snout, a long whip-like tail and tail spines. They give birth to live young.

Whitespotted Eagle Ray *Aetobatus ocellatus*

ID: 300cm wide. Grey with white spots and white belly.

HABITAT/RANGE: Coral reef or open water from central WA to northern NSW.

NOTES: Often form into schools and favour areas with currents.

COWNOSE RAYS (1 species)

Look very similar to eagle rays, except they have an indentation in the middle of the head. These medium-sized rays have a long tail and a small tail barb. Generally observed in large schools that can number in the hundreds, swimming in mid-water or at the surface. They feed on invertebrates and fish they dig from the sand, and are found in bays and estuaries and around reefs.

Australian Cownose Ray *Rhinoptera neglecta*

ID: 130cm wide. Brown to grey on dorsal surface.

HABITAT/RANGE: Reefs, bays and estuaries from northern WA to central NSW.

NOTES: Always seen in large schools, they seem to make seasonal movements along the east coast.

DEVILRAYS (5 species)

Most members of this family are very large, with a wide wing span and flap-like fins on the head that can be rolled to resemble horns. Devilrays mostly feed on plankton, which is sucked into their large mouth and filtered by gill rakers. These rays give birth to live young and five species are found around Australia.

Reef Manta Ray *Mobula alfredi*

ID: 500cm wide. Black dorsal surface with lighter patterns behind the head, and a white belly with black spots.

HABITAT/RANGE: Open water or coral reefs from central WA to northern NSW.

NOTES: These giant rays visit cleaning stations to have parasites removed. They have distinctive patterns of spots on their belly which can be used to identify individuals.

SNAKE EELS AND WORM EELS
(50 species)

These eels live in the sand by day and emerge at night to feed on fish and invertebrates. The snake eels have long snake-like bodies, and some even mimic the colour patterns of sea snakes, while worm eels are much smaller and thinner. Most bury in the sand tail first, and leave their head exposed. Found in tropical and temperate waters.

Serpent Eel *Ophisurus serpens*

ID: 250cm. Pale brown with a thin snout.

HABITAT/RANGE: Sandy bottoms from southern Qld to central WA.

NOTES: The heads of these large eels are sometimes seen by day, but they are far more active at night.

Longfinned Worm Eel *Scolecenchelys breviceps*

ID: 60cm. A small sandy-coloured eel.

HABITAT/RANGE: Sandy bottoms from southern NSW to southern WA.

NOTES: This shy species is not often seen, but it does emerge at night to eat shrimps.

MORAY EELS (c.85 species)

Morays have a reputation for being potentially dangerous, but they are quite docile and rarely bite unless hooked by an angler. They have this reputation because of their very sharp teeth and threatening look, even though one branch of the family has short blunt teeth design to crack the shells of crabs and molluscs. Morays eat a variety of fish and invertebrates, and live in recesses in the reef. Like other eels they spawn and the young drift with plankton until they settle on a reef. There are two types of morays: true morays that have a dorsal fin running the length of their body, and the rarer snakemorays that lack this fin and are more snake-like.

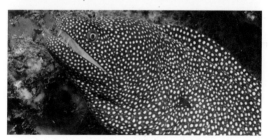

Whitemouth Moray *Gymnothorax meleagris*

ID: 120cm. Brown with white dots and a white mouth.

HABITAT/RANGE: Coral and rocky reef from central WA to NSW.

NOTES: Like many morays this species has decorative skin patterns that aid in camouflage on coral reefs.

Snowflake Moray *Echidna nebulosa*

ID: 100cm. White with black and yellow bands.

HABITAT/RANGE: Coral reefs off WA, Qld and northern NSW.

NOTES: Has blunt teeth and is often found in shallow bays with seagrass.

Barred Snakemoray *Uropterygius fasciolatus*

ID: 53cm. A brownish blotched eel with two nodules on the head.

HABITAT/RANGE: Coral reefs of the Great Barrier Reef.

NOTES: This rare and unusual moray has only been seen a few times.

CONGER EELS AND GARDEN EELS
(c.40 species)

These eels differ from morays by having small pectoral fins, large eyes and generally smaller teeth. Conger eels are large reef-dwelling eels that live in caves and recesses, while garden eels live in the sand in large colonies that can number in the thousands. Conger eels hunt for fish and crustaceans, while garden eels eat zooplankton.

Southern Conger Eel *Conger verreauxi*

ID: 220cm. Grey with thick lips.

HABITAT/RANGE: Rocky reefs from central NSW to western SA.

NOTES: A secretive eel that is not often seen.

Spotted Garden Eel *Heteroconger hassi*

ID: 60cm. White with black spots.

HABITAT/RANGE: Sand flats near coral reefs off Qld.

NOTES: These eels live in sandy areas and sway back and forth until a diver gets close, then they disappear into the sand.

EELTAIL CATFISHES (c.25 species)

Most catfish are confined to freshwater, with the eeltail catfishes also found in marine habitats. As the name suggests, these catfish have eel-like tails, but they also have cat-like whiskers (barbels) that help them to detect prey such as small fish and invertebrates. They are found in tropical and temperate waters and many have venomous spines for defence.

Estuary Catfish *Cnidoglanis macrocephalus*

ID: 91cm. Yellow or brown with darker blotches.

HABITAT/RANGE: Estuaries from southern Qld to southern WA, but absent from Tas and most of Vic.

NOTES: Usually hide under ledges by day and emerge at night to feed. Also called the Estuary Cobbler.

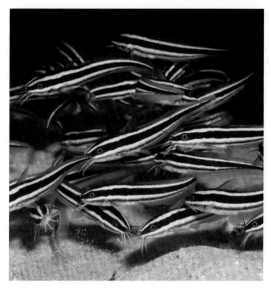

Striped Catfish *Plotosus lineatus*

ID: 35cm. Black-and-white stripes.

HABITAT/RANGE: Coral reefs from southern WA to central NSW.

NOTES: The most common catfish seen on coral reefs. Generally seen in large ball-like schools.

FLAGFINS (6 species)

Elongated bottom-dwelling fish that generally perch on the sea floor. Most live in deep water and are never seen, but a few live on shallow rocky reefs. They are ambush predators and grab fish and invertebrates that get close to them.

Sergeant Baker *Latropiscis purpurissatus*

ID: 60cm. Reddish with white blotches, bands and stripes.

HABITAT/RANGE: Rocky reefs from southern Qld to central WA.

NOTES: These large fish are seen sitting on the bottom, propped up by their large pectoral fins, waiting for unsuspecting prey.

LIZARDFISHES AND SAURIES
(c.30 species)

Sitting on the bottom and looking docile, lizardfishes and sauries fool most fish into thinking they are harmless. However, they are very effective predators with sharp teeth and fast reflexes, exploding from the bottom to grab small fish. These elongated fishes look very similar, just having different jaw structures and fins. Mostly found in tropical waters.

Variegated Lizardfish *Synodus variegatus*

ID: 40cm. Grey to red with six darker bands.

HABITAT/RANGE: Coral reefs from central WA to central NSW.

NOTES: This unassuming ambush predator often buries in the sand with only its eyes showing.

Clouded Saury *Saurida nebulosa*

ID: 19cm. Greyish with brown bands and blotches.

HABITAT/RANGE: Sandy bottoms or rubble off Qld and northern NSW.

NOTES: Sauries are generally not as colourful as lizardfish, which helps in camouflage on sandy bottoms.

TOADFISHES (9 species)

Also known as frogfish by some Australians, these strange bottom-dwelling fish have a flat head, a broad mouth and croak like a toad. Mainly feeding on small invertebrates, they live in caves and recesses, and are good parents, with the male looking after the eggs and young until they can fend for themselves.

Eastern Toadfish *Batrachomoeus dubius*

ID: 35cm. Grey with darker blotches and spots.

HABITAT/RANGE: Estuaries and bays from southern Qld to southern NSW.

NOTES: Often seen around Sydney and the only common toadfish in Australia, the other species being quite rare.

HANDFISHES (14 species)

Endemic to southern Australia, these strange bottom-dwelling fish walk across the bottom on hand-like fins. Most live in deep water and feed on crustaceans, molluscs and worms. All members of this family are under threat from habitat loss and invasive species eating their eggs.

Spotted Handfish *Brachionichthys hirsutus*

ID: 15cm. Creamy coloured with brown spots.

HABITAT/RANGE: Sandy bottoms in the Derwent Estuary, Tas.

NOTES: This is the best-known handfish, but it is critically endangered. A recovery plan is in action which aims to breed these unique fish.

FROGFISHES (c.30 species)

A small family of fishes within the larger anglerfish order Lophiiformes, which contains 16 families with head lures. Some people in Australia call members of this family anglerfish. Frogfish have decorative skin to camouflage them on the bottom so they can ambush fish and crustaceans. Like handfish, they also slowly walk across the bottom on modified fins. Many of the 30 or so species known from Australia are endemic.

Striate Frogfish *Antennarius striatus*

ID: 25cm. Can be yellow, white, brown or black, with darker stripes.

HABITAT/RANGE: Estuaries from central WA to central NSW.

NOTES: Often has hair-like filaments decorating its body, leading to it also being called the Hairy Frogfish.

ANTENNARIIDAE

Whitespotted Frogfish *Phyllophryne scortea*

ID: 10cm. Can be almost any colour with odd white spots.

HABITAT/RANGE: Rocky reefs from southern NSW to southern WA.

NOTES: This small frogfish likes to hide under rocks and old shells by day and feeds on gobies.

CLINGFISHES (c.43 species)

Easily overlooked as most are small, less than 5cm long, and cling to seaweed or coral, or hide on feather stars or sea urchins. These fish can cling to objects via modified ventral fins that act like a sucking cap. They mostly eat small invertebrates and zooplankton, and a few also clean other fish.

Tasmanian Clingfish *Aspasmogaster tasmaniensis*

ID: 8cm. Pink or pale brown with darker bands.

HABITAT/RANGE: Rocky reefs and bays from Vic to southern WA.

NOTES: A cryptic fish that hides under rocks and debris by day and emerges at night to feed.

BEARDIES (26 species)

This family also includes the deepsea cods, which are found in deep water, with the best-known members of the family being the beardies. These elongated fish have large eyes and chin barbels, and spend most of the day in caves or dark recesses. At night they feed on crustaceans, cephalopods and other fish. Three beardies are found in Australia, along with 23 deepsea cods.

Largetooth Beardie *Lotella rhacina*

ID: 66cm. Reddish-brown with white margins to the fins.

HABITAT/RANGE: Rocky reefs from southern Qld to southern WA.

NOTES: This secretive fish is often seen by divers as it shelters in caves.

PINEAPPLEFISHES (3 species)

These strange fishes have a hard exoskeleton that has the same pattern as a pineapple. They are slow swimming and hide in caves and under ledges by day. At night they roam rocky reefs looking for food with the aid of a bioluminescent organ below the eye. They mostly eat small shrimps.

Australian Pineapplefish *Cleidopus gloriamaris*

ID: 25cm. Yellow body with black hatching.

HABITAT/RANGE: Rocky reefs off southern Qld, throughout NSW and off southern WA.

NOTES: Often found in small groups hiding under ledges. They can use the same ledge for many years.

SQUIRRELFISHES AND SOLDIERFISHES
(34 species)

Nocturnal fishes with large eyes. Found in tropical waters, most are a reddish colour. They look very similar, with the squirrelfishes having a long sharp spine on their gill cover, while the soldierfishes have a short spine and a blunt head. Both form into schools and shelter in caves and under ledges by day. Squirrelfishes feed on small fish and invertebrates, while soldierfishes mostly eat zooplankton.

Whitetail Squirrelfish *Sargocentron caudimaculatum*

ID: 25cm. Has a red body with a white tail.

HABITAT/RANGE: Coral reefs off northern WA, eastern Qld and northern NSW.

NOTES: This distinctive member of the family feeds nocturnally on shrimps and crabs.

Blacktip Soldierfish *Myripristis botche*

ID: 30cm. Pale-coloured body with red edges to the scales and a red head and fins, with white margins to the fins and darker tips.

HABITAT/RANGE: Coral reefs off WA and Qld.

NOTES: Many soldierfish look very similar, so identifying species can be difficult.

NANNYGAIS AND RED SNAPPERS
(6 species)

The fish in this family have a forked tail and large eyes, as they feed at night on zooplankton. They are found in both deep and shallow water, and most species form into schools. Several species are fished commercially.

Swallowtail *Centroberyx lineatus*

ID: 36cm. Reddish-orange with a large red eye.

HABITAT/RANGE: Rocky reefs from southern NSW to central WA.

NOTES: This species mostly inhabits deeper water; only seen in shallow waters off southern WA.

FLUTEMOUTHES (2 species)

A very distinctive family of fish that have very elongated bodies, a long snout and a long tail filament. Often seen in loose schools, flutemouths feed on small fish and invertebrates that are sucked into their mouth.

Smooth Flutemouth *Fistularia commersonii*

ID: 170cm. Olive-green to light brown with blue dashes.

HABITAT/RANGE: Coral reefs from southern WA to central NSW.

NOTES: These fish mostly feed on the bottom, but will also stalk schools of small fish in mid-water.

TRUMPETFISHES (1 species)

Look very similar to flutemouthes, being elongated, but they have a more robust body and fins. Only found in tropical Australia, they feed on fish and crustaceans that are sucked into their tube-like snout.

Pacific Trumpetfish *Aulostomus chinensis*

ID: 90cm. There are two colour morphs: yellow or brown.

HABITAT/RANGE: Coral reefs from southern WA to central NSW.

NOTES: These ambush predators sneak up on prey and they often hide behind larger fish in order to do this.

SHRIMPFISHES (3 species)

Very thin-bodied fish that are shaped like an old cut-throat razor,
hence their other name of razorfish. Mostly seen in schools, they
move across the bottom in a vertical position with their head down.
Shrimpfish have a long tube-like snout and feed on zooplankton.

Rigid Shrimpfish *Centriscus scutatus*

ID: 15cm. Silvery with a reddish-brown stripe.

HABITAT/RANGE: Coral reefs from central WA to central Qld.

NOTES: Will swim in a horizontal position if fleeing predators and
often hides in black coral trees.

SEA MOTHS (4 species)

Small bottom-dwelling fish that look like a cross between a fish and a moth as their pectoral fins resemble wings. They have a rigid body case and walk across the bottom using modified ventral fins. A tube-like snout sucks up small crustaceans, worms and molluscs. Sea moths can shed their skin if it has algae growing on it.

Little Dragonfish *Eurypegasus draconis*

ID: 10cm. Cream or brownish with an intricate pattern.

HABITAT/RANGE: Sandy bottoms from southern WA to southern NSW.

NOTES: Often found in a male and female pair, with the male having blue margins on its pectoral fins.

GHOSTPIPEFISHES (5 species)

These small fish resemble pipefish, but have a shorter body and more elaborate fins. They are found in tropical waters feeding on small crustaceans that they suck into their mouth, which is at the end of a long snout. Ghostpipefish live near the bottom and have camouflaged skin patterns that help to conceal them. The female looks after the eggs in a pouched formed by the pelvic fins.

Robust Ghostpipefish *Solenostomus cyanopterus*

ID: 15cm. Can vary in colour from yellow to green to brown.

HABITAT/RANGE: Coral reefs and estuaries from central WA to central NSW.

NOTES: This species is often found in a male and female pair, with their colours matching nearby seaweeds.

SEAHORSES, PIPEHORSES, SEADRAGONS AND PIPEFISHES
(134 species)

Members of this large family share similar body features, but all look different. They all have a body protected by bony plates, a tube-like snout and the males look after the eggs, in either a brooding pouch or by sticking them to their tail. The groups differ from each other, with the pipefishes having an elongated body and head, while the others have their head at an angle to the body. Seahorses and pipehorses, and several pipefishes, also have prehensile tails to grip onto objects. These bottom-dwelling fish all feed on small crustaceans, mostly mysid shrimps. In total 28 seahorses, 11 pipehorses, 3 seadragons and 92 pipefish are found around Australia.

Bigbelly Seahorse
Hippocampus abdominalis

ID: 35cm. Varies in colour from cream to yellow to brown. Some have fleshy horns on their head.

HABITAT/RANGE: Rocky reefs from central NSW to western SA.

NOTES: This large seahorse is often seen by divers under jetties. They often stay in the same area for months and cling to sponges or seaweed.

Sydney Pygmy Pipehorse *Idiotropiscis lumnitzeri*

ID: 5.5cm. Reddish brown to purple with weed-like growths.

HABITAT/RANGE: Rocky reefs off NSW, from Sydney to Bawley Point.

NOTES: Groups of these tiny fish are often found clinging to one clump of algae. Sydney divers see them regularly in Botany Bay.

Leafy Seadragon *Phycodurus eques*

ID: 35cm. Yellow to orange-brown with leaf-like growths.

HABITAT/RANGE: Rocky reefs and bays from western Vic to southern WA.

NOTES: One of the most spectacular and sought-after fish in southern Australia, but often hard to find with its leaf-like camouflage.

Wide-body Pipefish *Stigmatopora nigra*

ID: 16cm. Green to brown with darker bands.

HABITAT/RANGE: Bays and estuaries from southern Qld to southern WA.

NOTES: This small pipefish is often hard to find as it clings to similar-coloured algae and seaweed.

SCORPIONFISHES (80 species)

This large and complex family contains fishes with venomous spines. Most species have camouflaged patterns and fleshy filaments to hide their presence so they can ambush prey, except for some lionfishes that have flamboyant feather-like fins they use to stalk prey. Scorpionfishes eat other fish and small invertebrates. Their toxic venom varies from species to species, with most causing intense pain and even death. If stung, immerse the wound in hot water and seek immediate medical treatment.

Eastern Red Scorpionfish *Scorpaena jacksoniensis*

ID: 40cm. Reddish with yellow or cream bands and blotches.

HABITAT/RANGE: Rocky reefs from southern Qld. to central Vic.

NOTES: Popular with anglers, these fish are slow growing and long lived, sometimes living more than 30 years.

Common Lionfish *Pterois volitans*

ID: 38cm. Long feather-like fins and a brown-and-white striped pattern.

HABITAT/RANGE: Coral reefs from southern WA to central NSW.

NOTES: Preys on small fish, using its fins to corral prey.

STINGFISHES AND STONEFISHES
(12 species)

Members of this family are closely related to the scorpionfishes, but have even more potent venom in their spines. These camouflaged fish have needle-sharp dorsal spines for defence, and most bury in sand or rubble by day. They are ambush predators that feed on fish and invertebrates.

Reef Stonefish   *Synanceia verrucosa*

ID: 40cm. Large body and short tail. Upturned snout and eyes. Colour varies from brown to pink.

HABITAT/RANGE: Reefs and estuaries from central WA to northern NSW.

NOTES: An antivenom is used to treat people stung by these well-camouflaged fish.

Demon Stingfish *Inimicus caledonicus*

ID: 25cm. Mottled brown, yellow or grey, with ragged fins.

HABITAT/RANGE: Rubble and sand from northern Qld to northern NSW.

NOTES: Known by many other names, including Demon Ghoul.

GURNARD PERCHES (14 species)

Another family with venomous spines. These temperate bottom-dwelling fish have a squarish head and a large mouth and eyes, plus spines on the head and gills. By day they hide under ledges, among seaweed or under a layer of sand. They feed at night on small fish and invertebrates.

Common Gurnard Perch
Neosebastes scorpaenoides

ID: 40cm. Cream to brown with darker bands.

HABITAT/RANGE: Rocky reefs and bays from central NSW to western SA.

NOTES: These large fish are often caught and eaten.

FORTESCUES AND WASPFISHES
(19 species)

Small, camouflaged, bottom-dwelling fishes with venomous dorsal spines and additional spines on their gill covers and below the eye. They feed on small invertebrates and fishes.

Eastern Fortescue *Centropogon australis*

ID: 14cm. Creamy colour with darker blotches and spots.

HABITAT/RANGE: Rocky reefs from southern Qld to Vic and northern Tas.

NOTES: A small fish, often found in groups in estuary habitats.

Blackspot Waspfish *Liocranium praepositum*

ID: 13cm. Orange to brown with darker fins and a large black spot behind the head.

HABITAT/RANGE: Coral reefs and bays off Qld.

NOTES: A little-known species that is common in Brisbane's Moreton Bay.

VELVETFISHES (20 species)

Closely related to the scorpionfish, they have a single dorsal fin that runs the length of the body. These bottom-dwelling fish are highly camouflaged and have venomous spines. Velvetfish have rough leather-like skin. They ambush prey, feeding on small fish and invertebrates.

Mossback Velvetfish *Paraploactis trachyderma*

ID: 30cm. Varies in colour from grey to yellow, often with blotched patterns.

HABITAT/RANGE: Bays and estuaries from western NT to central NSW.

NOTES: These cryptic fish are found on sandy bottoms and camouflage in seaweed and among sponges.

PROWFISHES (3 species)

Look similar to waspfishes and velvetfishes in having a long extended dorsal fin, but these scaleless fish have large pectoral fins and lack pelvic fins. They are bottom-dwelling fish that are only found in southern Australia. Most look like a sponge, and they use concealment to catch small crustaceans.

Red Indianfish *Pataecus fronto*

ID: 27cm. Orange or red with a high dorsal fin.

HABITAT/RANGE: Rocky reefs off southern Qld, NSW and parts of SA and WA.

NOTES: These strange fish are often found in pairs. Like all prowfish, they regularly shed their skin in order to grow and to remove algal growth.

RED VELVETFISH (1 species)

The only member of its family, the Red Velvetfish has large rounded
fins and a velvet-like skin. This bottom-dwelling fish is found on
rocky reefs with a dense coverage of seaweed and kelp. They are
ambush predators, feeding at night on crustaceans and small fish.
Their spines are also venomous.

Red Velvetfish *Gnathanacanthus goetzeei*

ID: 46cm. Red with white blotches.

HABITAT/RANGE: Rocky reefs from eastern Vic to southern WA.

NOTES: A very cryptic fish that hides among seaweed and kelp by
day.

FLYING GURNARDS (4 species)

A family of fish with oversized and colourful 'wings', which are actually enlarged pectoral fins. While they don't allow the fish to fly over the waves like a flying fish, they may be used to startle potential predators. Flying gurnards are bottom-dwelling fish that 'walk' slowly across the bottom on their modified pelvic fins. They feed on small fish, crustaceans and molluscs.

Oriental Flying Gurnard *Dactyloptena orientalis*

ID: 40cm. Creamy coloured with brown spots and blue stripes on the 'wings'.

HABITAT/RANGE: Sandy bottoms from central WA to southern NSW.

NOTES: The 'wings' on this species are folded along the body and only open when fleeing a predator.

GURNARDS (35 species)

The gurnards have smaller pectoral fins than the flying gurnards, and have a head armoured with bony plates. These bottom-dwelling fish are mostly found on sandy bottoms, often in deep water, where they prey on small fish, cephalopods and crustaceans at night. Their wings are brightly coloured and are displayed to warn off predators.

Spiny Gurnard *Lepidotrigla papilio*

ID: 20cm. Cream or red body with blotches and an eye spot.

HABITAT/RANGE: Sandy bays from southern Qld to southern WA.

NOTES: This species varies greatly in colour, depending on the area, which led to it originally being described as several different species.

FLATHEADS (52 species)

A well-represented family in Australia, these bottom-dwelling fish have a flattened elongated body and a triangular-shaped head. They often bury in the sand with only their eyes exposed, and ambush prey that includes small fish, cephalopods and crustaceans. Most tropical species are small and remain hidden by day, while the temperate species are much larger and often active by day. A number of species are taken by anglers.

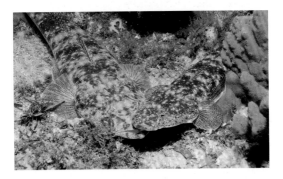

Dusky Flathead *Platycephalus fuscus*

ID: 120cm. Sandy-brown with darker blotches and white spots.

HABITAT/RANGE: Sandy bottoms from northern Qld to eastern Vic.

NOTES: Often seen in pairs, with a small male snuggling up to a much larger female.

ROCKCODS, GROPERS AND BASSLETS
(c.190 species)

This large and complex family contains fishes both big and small that typically have a robust compressed body, a large mouth and gills with small spines. Many subfamilies are contained in Serranidae, including rockcods, coral trouts, gropers, wirrahs, basslets, seaperch, perch and soapfish. All members have sharp teeth and most are ambush predators feeding on fish and invertebrates, except for the basslets and perch that feed on zooplankton. Many species are protogynous hermaphrodites, starting life as females and changing to males later in life. Most species are tropical.

Bar-cheek Coral Trout *Plectropomus maculatus*

ID: 125cm. Red to brown with blue spots. Elongated spots on head.

HABITAT/RANGE: Coral reefs from central WA to southern Qld.

NOTES: Like all coral trout this is a popular fish with anglers.

Harlequin Fish *Othos dentex*

ID: 86cm. Orange to pink with blue and green spots.

HABITAT/RANGE: Rocky reefs with seaweed from eastern SA to central WA.

NOTES: One of the few temperate rockcods, these fish sit on the bottom and ambush prey.

White-lined Rockcod

White-lined Rockcod *Anyperodon leucogrammicus*

ID: 65cm. Pale brown with white lines and orange spots.

HABITAT/RANGE: Coral reefs from central WA and central Qld.

NOTES: Like other rockcods, this is a bottom-dwelling fish that hides under ledges.

Potato Cod *Epinephelus tukula*

ID: 200cm. Greyish-white with black blotches.

HABITAT/RANGE: Coral reefs from central WA to southern Qld.

NOTES: A large groper that hides in caves. Some have been tamed by divers and are hand fed.

Butterfly Perch *Caesioperca lepidoptera*

ID: 30cm. Pinkish body with dark blotch on side.

HABITAT/RANGE: Rocky reefs from northern NSW to southern WA.

NOTES: Seen in large schools in areas with currents.

Orange Basslet.

Orange Basslet *Pseudanthias squamipinnis*

ID: 15cm male is purple-pink, 7cm female is orange.

HABITAT/RANGE: Coral and rocky reefs from northern Qld to central NSW.

NOTES: Males have a harem of females. Feeds in the current.

Barred Soapfish *Diploprion bifasciatum*

ID: 25cm. Yellow and grey body with yellow fins.

HABITAT/RANGE: Coral reefs from central WA to northern NSW.

NOTES: Soapfish hide in caves and have a toxic skin that lathers like soap.

DOTTYBACKS (38 species)

Small reef fish with elongated bodies and pupils. Found in northern Australia, they are quite secretive, hiding in holes and under ledges, but many are also territorial and aggressive towards other small fish. They eat small fish and invertebrates.

Longtail Dottyback *Oxycercichthys veliferus*

ID: 12cm. Pale grey to yellow with blue bands across eyes.

HABITAT/RANGE: Coral reefs of the Great Barrier Reef.

NOTES: Many dottybacks have bright colours, while the Longtail Dottyback has more subdued colours.

LONGFINS (25 species)

A diverse group that contains the scissortails, hulafish and blue
devils. These fish may look different, but they share similar
characteristics of an elongated body, large eyes, a single dorsal fin
and enlarged pelvic fins. Most species live on the bottom, often in
caves, and the hulafish are typically seen in schools. The smaller
members of this family feed on plankton, while the blue devils eat
a variety of invertebrates.

Yellow Scissortail *Assessor flavissimus*

ID: 6cm. Yellow with orange stripes on the fins.

HABITAT/RANGE: Caves and ledges on the Great Barrier Reef.

NOTES: A secretive cave fish. The male broods the eggs in its
mouth.

Yellowhead Hulafish *Trachinops noarlungae*

ID: 15cm. Greyish body with a yellow head and tail.

HABITAT/RANGE: Rocky reefs from eastern SA to southern WA.

NOTES: Groups of these small fish are often found under jetties.

Southern Blue Devil *Paraplesiops meleagris*

ID: 35cm. Dark blue colour with bright blue spots.

HABITAT/RANGE: Rocky reefs from eastern Vic to southern WA.

NOTES: Often sits on the bottom, propped up on its fins. Long lived, reaching at least 60 years of age.

PEARLPERCHES (4 species)

Deep-bodied silvery-coloured fish with an elevated rear dorsal fin and large eyes. Most species live in deep water, often in schools, but a few also venture into shallow water. They eat small fish and invertebrates. Popular with anglers.

Threadfin Pearl Perch *Glaucosoma magnificum*

ID: 32cm. Silver with vertical bands and long threads on the fins.

HABITAT/RANGE: Coral reefs from central WA to central Qld.

NOTES: Mostly seen off WA in tight-packed schools.

GRUNTERS (c.40 species)

Most fish use their swim bladder to maintain neutral buoyancy, while some, like the grunters, also use it to make noises. These silver-coloured fish have an ovate body shape and two spines on their gill cover. Most are seen in schools on reefs or in estuaries, and a number are found in freshwater. They feed on the bottom on small invertebrates.

Eastern Striped Grunter *Pelates sexlineatus*

ID: 20cm. Silver with six dark stripes.

HABITAT/RANGE: Reefs and estuaries from southern Qld to southern NSW.

NOTES: Often hide in seaweed and seagrass.

FLAGTAILS (3 species)

A small family of fish that are nearly always seen in schools. They have a small elongated body with a forked tail, are silver in colour, with most having darker bands or spots on their tail. Flagtails inhabit shallow reefs and estuaries, and have large eyes to feed at night on zooplankton and small fish.

Fivebar Flagtail *Kuhlia mugil*

ID: 32cm. Silver with black and white bands on tail.

HABITAT/RANGE: Shallows tropical waters from northern WA to central NSW.

NOTES: This species is often caught by fishers to use as bait.

WHITINGS (13 species)

Elongated silvery fish that are popular with anglers. Most species are found in schools over sandy bottoms. They dig most of their prey out of the sand, and feed on a range of small invertebrate species.

Stout Whiting *Sillago robusta*

ID: 50cm. Silver with yellow blotch on cheek.

HABITAT/RANGE: Sandy bottoms off Qld, northern NSW and central WA.

NOTES: Generally found in deep water. Taken by recreational and commercial fishers.

BIGEYES (10 species)

Named for their rather large eyes, these nocturnal fish are mostly red in colour, but can change to silver or a blotched pattern. They have a compressed body and a projecting lower jaw. By day most are seen in caves or under ledges, often in small groups. At night they feed in mid-water on zooplankton and small fish.

Lunartail Bigeye *Priacanthus hamrur*

ID: 40cm. Usually reddish, but often silver with red bands.

HABITAT/RANGE: Coral reefs from central WA to central NSW.

NOTES: Mostly hidden during daytime, but schools sometimes swarm over reefs by day.

CARDINALFISHES (c.150 species)

Small reef-dwelling fishes that live in caves and under ledges. Their features include a small compressed body, two dorsal fins and a large eye close to the snout. These nocturnal fish emerge at night to feed on small crustaceans, fish and plankton. Mostly found in shallow tropical waters, many are seen in schools and they are mouth brooders.

Ringtailed Cardinalfish *Ostorhinchus aureus*

ID: 14.5cm. Copper coloured with a black band at the base of the tail and blue stripes on face.

HABITAT/RANGE: Coral reefs from central WA to central NSW.

NOTES: A common tropical species, but easily confused with many similar cardinalfish.

Sydney Cardinalfish *Ostorhinchus limenus*

ID: 14cm. Silver-grey body with five dark stripes and pink fins.

HABITAT/RANGE: Rocky reefs from southern Qld to central Vic.

NOTES: This temperate species is best seen in estuaries and bays.
Fish with swollen jaws are usually holding eggs in their mouth.

BLANQUILLOS AND TILEFISHES
(10 species)

These elongated slender fish all have a small head, a spine on their gill cover and single extended dorsal and anal fins. The main difference between them is that tilefishes are small and feed on zooplankton and blanquillos are larger and feed on small invertebrates. Found in tropical waters, both are bottom-dwelling, often seen in pairs and have burrows in the sand or rubble.

Flagtail Blanquillo *Malacanthus brevirostris*

ID: 32cm. Greyish with a yellowish head and faint bars and black stripes on the tail.

HABITAT/RANGE: Sandy bottoms from northern WA to central NSW.

NOTES: A shy fish that dives into its burrow when disturbed.

Bluehead Tilefish *Hoplolatilus starcki*

ID: 15cm. Yellowish-cream body and blue head.

HABITAT/RANGE: Sand and rubble off northern Great Barrier Reef.

NOTES: A rarely seen fish. Usually in pairs when spotted.

COBIA (1 species)

The only member of its family, this elongated fish has well-formed fins that make it look like a shark. Cobia eat other fish and a variety of invertebrates, and mostly feed on the bottom. They are seen in schools or alone, and often rest on the bottom, but are also observed in mid-water or near the surface. Cobia look very similar to remoras, and while they can't attach to other fishes, they do like to swim with larger species such as Whale Sharks and Reef Manta Rays.

Cobia *Rachycentron canadum*

ID: 200cm. Black with a white stripe.

HABITAT/RANGE: Reef and sand from southern WA to southern NSW.

NOTES: Popular with anglers.

REMORAS (7 species)

Elongated fish with a modified dorsal fin that acts like a suction cap and allows them to attach to large animals such as sharks, rays and other fishes, turtles and whales. Almost parasitic, remoras do provide some cleaning duties to their host. They steal scraps from their host and eat small fish.

Slender Suckerfish *Echeneis naucrates*

ID: 110cm. White with a thick black stripe.

HABITAT/RANGE: Tropical and temperate waters around Australia.

NOTES: Groups can attach to sharks, and often the host will scrape along the bottom to try to dislodge them.

TREVALLIES (69 species)

A large and complex family that also includes the darts, scads, kingfish, amberjacks and queenfish. All these fish typically have an oblong-shaped compressed body with a strong forked tail and a lateral line with raised spiny scales. Mostly seen in schools swimming in mid-water. They feed on zooplankton or small fish depending on their size.

Yellowtail Kingfish *Seriola lalandi*

ID: 250cm. Elongated bullet-shaped fish. Silver with a yellow stripe and yellow fins.

HABITAT/RANGE: Rocky reefs from southern Qld to central WA.

NOTES: Popular game fish that is also farmed.

Southern Yellowtail Scad *Trachurus novaezelandiae*

ID: 50cm. Silver with a yellow tail and dorsal fin.

HABITAT/RANGE: Rocky reefs from southern Qld to central WA.

NOTES: Seen in large schools, often under jetties. Individuals over 30cm long rarely encountered.

Bigeye Trevally *Caranx sexfasciatus*

ID: 78cm. Silver with white tips to the median fins.

HABITAT/RANGE: Coral reefs from central WA to northern NSW.

NOTES: A very common trevally seen in large schools.

MACKERELS AND TUNAS (26 species)

These fishes have elongated, streamlined bodies with powerful forked tails. Other members of the family include the bonitos and Wahoo. Features include a pointed head, silvery scales, sharp teeth and finlets between the rear fins and the tail. Most are pelagic, being seen in mid-water or near the surface, but quite a few visit reefs to feed. These fast-moving species feed on small fishes and some invertebrates.

Shark Mackerel *Grammatorcynus bicarinatus*

ID: 130cm. Silvery-blue with black spots on the belly.

HABITAT/RANGE: Tropical waters from central WA to northern NSW.

NOTES: Seen in schools or singly. Will sometimes venture over reef flats at high tide to capture prey.

Southern Bluefin Tuna *Thunnus maccoyii*

ID: 225cm. Dark grey dorsal surface, white belly and yellow tail and finlets.

HABITAT/RANGE: Open waters from northern NSW to northern WA.

NOTES: Highly prized fish that can maintain a higher core body temperature than the cooler surrounding waters.

SILVERBELLIES (10 species)

Small fishes with silver scales, a short-compressed body and a projecting snout. These bottom-feeding species are mostly seen over sand, where they prey on small invertebrates. Often seen in schools.

Silverbelly *Parequula melbournensis*

ID: 22cm. Silver with a bluish tinge and yellow margins to the fins.

HABITAT/RANGE: Sand and seagrass from southern Qld to southern WA.

NOTES: This species can be seen alone or in schools.

THREADFIN BREAMS AND MONOCLE BREAMS (37 species)

Found in tropical Australia, they typically have a slender to ovate body with a single dorsal fin and most have colourful stripes. Threadfin breams have tail filaments and monocle breams have a spine below the eye. Mostly seen on the bottom, swimming with a stop-start-hover motion when looking for prey of small fish and invertebrates.

Paradise Threadfin Bream *Pentapodus paradiseus*

ID: 30cm. Adult pale grey with bright blue and yellow stripes.

HABITAT/RANGE: Coral reefs from central NT to northern NSW.

NOTES: The juvenile of this species is very different with a bold black and yellow stripe.

Two-lined Monocle Bream *Scolopsis bilineata*

ID: 23cm. Lower body white, upper body black with yellow stripes.

HABITAT/RANGE: Coral reefs from central WA to northern NSW.

NOTES: Common on coral reefs, these small fish are protogynous hermaphrodites, changing sex from female to male.

EMPERORS (32 species)

Emperors vary greatly in size, although they all have an oblong compressed body, large eyes positioned on the forehead and thick lips. These fish are bottom-dwellers that feed on invertebrates grabbed from the sand. Almost all species are tropical.

Red-throated Emperor *Lethrinus miniatus*

ID: 90cm. Greyish-brown body, often blotched, with a reddish head.

HABITAT/RANGE: Coral reefs and sand from central WA to northern NSW.

NOTES: This and many other emperors are popular with anglers, but many contain ciguatera poison.

SNAPPER AND BREAMS (12 species)

Almost all members of this family are popular with anglers. These silver-coloured fish have an oblong compressed body and a rounded forehead. Most are seen in schools and all feed on the bottom at night on small fish and invertebrates.

Snapper *Chrysophrys auratus*

ID: 130cm. Silvery-pink with blue specks. Large fish have head hump.

HABITAT/RANGE: Rocky reefs from central Qld. to central WA.

NOTES: Important commercial species that can live to 40 years of age.

Yellowfin Bream *Acanthopagrus australis*

ID: 66cm. Silver body with yellow pelvic and anal fins and a black margin on the tail and dorsal fin.

HABITAT/RANGE: Bays and estuaries from central Qld to central Vic.

NOTES: These bream spawn around river mouths, with the young developing in mangroves and estuaries.

SWEETLIPS (21 species)

Easily recognised by their very thick lips. Most also have colourful patterns and an oblong-shaped compressed body. Sweetlips feed at night on small invertebrates, and by day they either form into hovering schools or linger under ledges. The juveniles have oversized fins and bold colours and never stop moving across the bottom.

Oblique-banded Sweetlips *Plectorhinchus lineatus*

ID: 72cm. White with diagonal black stripes on upper body and yellow fins and lips.

HABITAT/RANGE: Coral reefs from northern WA to central Qld.

NOTES: Groups of these colourful fish hover on coral heads with their heads pointing into the current.

CORAL SNAPPERS (54 species)

Mostly found in tropical waters, these fishes have an ovate to elongated compressed body and a single dorsal fin that is notched. Often identified by their colourful patterns. Generally observed in schools, but sometimes solitary or seen in pairs. Most species feed on small fishes or invertebrates at night.

Red Emperor Snapper *Lutjanus sebae*

ID: 116cm. White with three red bands.

HABITAT/RANGE: Coral reefs from central WA to northern NSW.

NOTES: This pretty fish is popular with anglers, but they are known to carry ciguatera.

Blue-striped Snapper *Lutjanus kasmira*

ID: 40cm. Yellow body with four blue stripes.

HABITAT/RANGE: Coral reefs from central WA to central NSW.

NOTES: Always seen in schools.

FUSILIERS (13 species)

Small tropical fish with a slender body, forked tail and single dorsal fin. The eyes are very close to their small mouth. Always seen in schools, swimming close to the bottom or in mid-water and feeding on plankton. At night they hide in coral or under ledges.

Blue-and-yellow Fusilier *Caesio teres*

ID: 40cm. Blue with a yellow tail and rear back.

HABITAT/RANGE: Coral reefs off northern WA and northern Qld.

NOTES: Not a common fusilier. Mostly seen on remote reefs.

JEWFISHES (18 species)

Can produce drum-like sounds, which has led to some being called drums or croakers. They produce this unique sound with the abdominal muscles beating against the swim bladder. These elongated fish have small scales and a long dorsal fin, and are found in deep water, freshwater and estuaries. They feed on small fishes and invertebrates.

Mulloway *Argyrosomus japonicus*

ID: 200cm. Silvery with white spots along the lateral line.

HABITAT/RANGE: Bays, estuaries and rocky reefs from southern Qld to central WA.

NOTES: Often seen in schools. A popular fish with anglers.

GOATFISHES (39 species)

Bottom-dwelling fishes that grub in the sand with two long chin barbels to find prey such as small invertebrates. Found mostly in tropical Australia, these elongated fish generally have colourful skin patterns. Some species school and others are seen in small groups or individually.

Blacksaddle Goatfish *Parupeneus spilurus*

ID: 55cm. White and brown stripes with a black saddle spot near tail, and many bright blue highlights.

HABITAT/RANGE: Rocky reefs from southern Qld to eastern Vic and southern WA.

NOTES: One of the largest goatfish. At night they rest on the bottom and their colours become dull.

BULLSEYES (16 species)

These small nocturnal fish have big eyes, a short-compressed body, a short snout and projecting lower jaw. By day they hide under ledges and in caves, often in schools, emerging at night to feed on small invertebrates and fishes.

Blacktip Bullseye *Pempheris affinis*

ID: 15cm. Gold or silver with black tips to the fins.

HABITAT/RANGE: Rocky reefs from southern Qld to eastern Vic.

NOTES: Many bullseyes look very similar with only subtle differences between them.

ARCHERFISHES (4 species)

Found in northern Australia, they have one of the most unique hunting methods of any fish, as they squirt water at insects perched on mangrove branches to knock them into the water. To achieve this feat, they have eyes near the top of their head, so they can look up. These small silver-coloured fish are found in estuaries and creeks.

Banded Archerfish *Toxotes jaculatrix*

ID: 30cm. Silver with darker bands.

HABITAT/RANGE: Mangroves from northern WA to central Qld.

NOTES: Archerfishes also feed on floating vegetation.

POMFREDS (3 species)

The members of this family have pointed dorsal and anal fins that give these fish a diamond-like shape. These small silvery fish are usually found in schools and mostly eat zooplankton and algae.

Eastern Pomfred *Schuettea scalaripinnis*

ID: 20cm. Silver body with yellow fins.

HABITAT/RANGE: Bays and estuaries from southern Qld to southern NSW.

NOTES: A nocturnal species that shelters under ledges and jetties by day.

SWEEPS (6 species)

Small oval-shaped fish with forked tails and triangular dorsal and anal fins. Occurring in Australia's temperate waters, they are usually found in schools swimming in mid-water and feeding on zooplankton and algae.

Sea Sweep *Scorpis aequipinnis*

ID: 48cm. Silver with two faint bands.

HABITAT/RANGE: Rocky reefs from southern NSW to central WA.

NOTES: Found in a variety of habitats, even the surf zone where waves break onto rocks.

DRUMMERS (7 species)

Very similar to the sweeps, except larger and mostly found in tropical waters. They typically have a small head, eyes and mouth and graze on algae and small invertebrates. Almost always seen in schools.

Grey Drummer *Kyphosus bigibbus*

ID: 75cm. Grey body with darker fins.

HABITAT/RANGE: Coral reefs from central WA to central NSW.

NOTES: This species is found around the world and often seen in the wave zone on coral reefs.

BLACKFISHES (5 species)

The blackfishes look very similar to the drummers, but have a different fin arrangement and mouth structure. They are mostly found in temperate waters, and feed on algae nibbled off rocks and small invertebrates. Only found in southern Australia, blackfishes are popular with anglers and are mostly found in schools on rocky reefs.

Luderick *Girella tricuspidata*

ID: 70cm. Grey with darker stripes.

HABITAT/RANGE: Rocky reefs from southern Qld to central SA.

NOTES: Common in estuaries. Spawns mostly at river mouths or in the surf zone.

STRIPEYS (6 species)

The stripeys are oval-shaped fish with striped patterns and a spikey dorsal fin. These small fish are often found in schools and feed on the bottom on small invertebrates and plankton.

East Australian Stripey *Microcanthus joyceae*

ID: 11cm. Yellow body with black bands.

HABITAT/RANGE: Rocky reefs from central Qld to southern NSW.

NOTES: The very similar-looking Stripey (Microcanthus strigatus) is found off WA.

Moonlighter *Tilodon sexfasciatus*

ID: 40cm. Silver body with black bands.

HABITAT/RANGE: Rocky reefs from central Vic to southern WA.

NOTES: Unlike other stripeys, these fish are seen singly or in pairs.

BUTTERFLYFISHES (63 species)

Some of the prettiest and most colourful fish in the sea. They are oval shaped with a compressed body, a small mouth on a pointed snout, and almost symmetrical dorsal and anal fins. Most feed on small invertebrates, but others eat zooplankton. Most butterflyfish live in tropical waters, although some also venture into warm temperate zones, and a few are found only in temperate waters. Many are seen in pairs, while others form into schools. Talma, coralfish and bannerfish are included within the family.

Western Talma *Chelmonops curiosus*

ID: 26cm. Silver with black bands.

HABITAT/RANGE: Rocky reefs from eastern SA to southern WA.

NOTES: Feed on small worms and crustaceans. The similar-looking Eastern Talma (Chelmonops truncatus) is found off NSW.

Beaked Coralfish *Chelmon rostratus*

ID: 20cm. Elongated snout, silver colour with orange bands with black trim and a black eye-spot.

HABITAT/RANGE: Coral reefs from northern Qld to central NSW.

NOTES: Butterflyfish are pelagic spawners, with their eggs and young drifting with ocean currents, which allows species like this to be found in temperate areas of NSW.

Threadfin Butterflyfish *Chaetodon auriga*

ID: 23cm. White body, yellow back and tail, and a darker cross-hatch pattern.

HABITAT/RANGE: Coral and rocky reefs from southern WA to southern NSW.

NOTES: Always seen in a male/female pair that patrol their home range.

Schooling Bannerfish *Heniochus diphreutes*

ID: 21cm. White with black bands and yellow fins.

HABITAT/RANGE: Coral reefs from central WA to central NSW.

NOTES: This species has a long banner-like filament off its dorsal fin and is always seen in schools.

Threadfin Butterflyfish

ANGELFISHES (36 species)

Some small angelfish look similar to butterflyfish, but differ in having a prominent spine on their gill cover. These colourful fish feed on a variety of things, including zooplankton, sponges, coral polyps and small invertebrates. Larger angelfish are always seen in male/female pairs, while smaller angelfish are seen in groups comprising a male and his harem of females. Angelfish are mostly found in tropical waters, with a few ranging into warm temperate waters.

Emperor Angelfish *Pomacanthus imperator*

ID: 38cm. Blue with yellow stripes and a black face mask.

HABITAT/RANGE: Coral reefs from central WA to northern NSW.

NOTES: The young of large angelfish have very different colour patterns, this one being blue with white bands and rings.

Bicolor Angelfish *Centropyge bicolor*

ID: 15cm. Half yellow and half blue.

HABITAT/RANGE: Coral reefs from central WA to northern NSW.

NOTES: One of the pygmy angelfish, where a female can change sex to male if the dominant male dies.

Male.

Female.

Swallowtail Angelfish *Genicanthus melanospilos*

ID: 18cm. Male grey with black stripes, female yellowish-grey with black stripes on tail.

HABITAT/RANGE: Coral reefs of the northern Great Barrier Reef.

NOTES: Most angelfish have the same colours for males and females, except for this species and several other angelfish with swallow-like tails.

144

DAMSELFISHES (161 species)

A large and complex family of small fish that have a rounded compressed body, a small mouth and a single continuous dorsal fin. Many are brightly coloured. Within the family are scalyfins, gregories, pullers, humbugs, sergeants, demoiselles, chromis and anemonefishes. They all have slight differences in body shape and fins that set them apart. Damselfishes are bottom-dwellers that feed on a variety of foods, including plankton, algae and small invertebrates.

Damselfishes are good parents, and deposit eggs on the bottom, where they are guarded by the male until they hatch. The female damselfish is often the dominant partner, and if she dies the male can change sex to take her place.

Headbang Humbug *Dascyllus reticulatus*

ID: 9cm long, light brown body with darker fins and band behind the gills.

HABITAT/RANGE: Coral reefs off WA and northern Qld to northern NSW.

NOTES: Always found in groups, living in branching hard corals.

Scalyfin *Parma victoriae*

ID: 25cm. Adult has a grey, brown or black body with white spots on the lateral line. Juvenile bright yellow with blue lines.

HABITAT/RANGE: Temperate rocky reefs from central Vic to southern WA.

NOTES: Adults are very territorial when breeding and will attack other fish and divers.

Golden Damsel *Amblyglyphidodon aureus*

ID: 13cm. Golden-yellow with blue around the eyes.

HABITAT/RANGE: Coral reefs off northern WA and northern Qld.

NOTES: These damsels eat zooplankton and hang around gorgonian fans, where they lay their eggs.

Coral Sea Gregory *Plectroglyphidodon gascoynei*

ID: 15cm. Greyish with a yellow belly and eyes.

HABITAT/RANGE: Coral reefs from central Qld. to central NSW.

NOTES: Like most damselfishes, this species lays its eggs on the bottom and they are guarded by the male.

Eastern Clown Anemonefish.

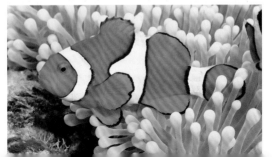

Blackhead Puller *Chromis klunzingeri*

ID: 6.5cm. White with a yellow back and black patch on the head.

HABITAT/RANGE: Rocky reefs off south-west corner of WA.

NOTES: Most damselfishes are found in tropical waters, but a good variety occur in southern Australia, including this species.

Eastern Clown Anemonefish *Amphiprion percula*

ID: 11cm. Orange with white bands with black borders.

HABITAT/RANGE: Coral reefs off northern to central Qld.

NOTES: Anemonefish live in sea anemones and have a coating on their skin that stops them from getting stung.

BATFISHES (6 species)

The batfishes have a compressed oval shaped body with well-developed dorsal and anal fins. Juveniles have oversized fins and ornate patterns, while the adults have a silvery colour with dark bands. Found mainly in tropical waters, most batfish are seen in schools, either hanging in mid-water, near the surface or close to the bottom. They feed on small invertebrates and zooplankton.

Roundface Batfish *Platax teira*

ID: 70cm. Silver-grey with darker bands and yellow pectoral fins.

HABITAT/RANGE: Coral reefs from southern WA to central NSW.

NOTES: This species is often found in temperate waters, and the juveniles look like brown leaves.

BOARFISHES (10 species)

The temperate equivalent of a batfish, but with an elongated snout, large eyes and a spiny dorsal fin. Found in southern Australia on rocky reefs in shallow and deep water. Boarfishes shelter in caves and ledges by day, emerging at night to feed on worms, brittlestars and other small invertebrates.

Longsnout Boarfish *Pentaceropsis recurvirostris*

ID: 50cm. Silvery white with black bands.

HABITAT/RANGE: Rocky reefs from central NSW to southern WA.

NOTES: A common species often seen by divers. It is thought that its fins may be venomous.

OLD WIFE (1 species)

With long fins and a pointed snout, the Old Wife is the only member of its family. At one time it was listed as a type of butterflyfish, but it appears to be more closely related to the boarfish. Generally seen in schools, hovering over reef, seaweed or under jetties. These fish feed on small invertebrates.

Old Wife *Enoplosus armatus*

ID: 30cm. Silver with black or brown bands.

HABITAT/RANGE: Rocky reefs from southern Qld to central WA.

NOTES: A very common fish that is well known to divers, but avoid its fin spines as they carry venom.

MORWONGS (14 species)

Often seen perched on the bottom on their long pectoral fins, the morwongs are common throughout the temperate waters of Australia. These elongated, triangular-shaped fish have a high forehead, a forked tail and small thick lips. Most species have colourful skin patterns. Bottom feeders, they eat small invertebrates mostly grabbed from the sand. Seen either singly or in groups.

Red-lip Morwong *Goniistius rubrolabiatus*

ID: 40cm. White with reddish-brown bands and dots and red lips.

HABITAT/RANGE: Rocky reefs off the south-west corner of WA.

NOTES: One of the most colourful and highly decorated members of the family.

TRUMPETERS (3 species)

The trumpeters and morwongs are closely related and some place them in the same family. However, the trumpeters are more elongated and have small rounded pectoral fins. Only occurring in southern Australia, and generally found in schools close to the bottom, these fish feed on small invertebrates and sometimes plankton.

Bastard Trumpeter *Latridopsis forsteri*

ID: 70cm. Silver base colour with orange stripes.

HABITAT/RANGE: Rocky reefs from central NSW to central SA.

NOTES: Found in schools grubbing on the bottom for food. A popular fish with anglers.

MULLETS (23 species)

Elongated fish with a broad depressed head, two widely spaced dorsal fins, a small mouth and large silver scales. Mostly seen in schools, mullet feed on the bottom by grabbing mouthfuls of sand and filtering out edible detritus. Many mullets are fished and farmed.

Wartylip Mullet *Crenimugil crenilabis*

ID: 60cm. Silvery-green with stripes along the scale rows.

HABITAT/RANGE: Reefs and sandy areas from northern Qld to northern NSW.

NOTES: Often seen in lagoons on the Great Barrier Reef.

BARRACUDAS (12 species)

Predatory fish that feast on other fishes. With powerful forked tails, and long canine-like teeth, these elongated fish stalk and attack other fish with a quick turn of speed. These silver-coloured fish are mostly found in tropical waters, generally in schools, and are free swimming in mid-water, often close to reefs or pinnacles.

Great Barracuda *Sphyraena barracuda*

ID: 200cm. Silver with faint bars and darker coloured fins.

HABITAT/RANGE: Coral reefs from central WA to northern NSW.

NOTES: These barracuda are solitary fish that are popular with anglers.

SEACARPS (4 species)

Hiding on the bottom among the seaweed and kelp, seacarps are cryptic temperate fishes found only in southern Australia, inhabiting shallow rocky reefs and feeding on seaweeds and algae. They have an elongated body, a rounded head, a notched dorsal fin and a mottled skin pattern to aid with camouflage.

Rock Cale *Aplodactylus lophodon*

ID: 45cm. Grey with darker blotches and five white dashes on body.

HABITAT/RANGE: Rocky reefs from southern Qld to eastern Vic.

NOTES: Often found in the intertidal zone.

KELPFISHES (4 species)

Kelpfishes are very similar to the seacarps with an elongated body and a mottled skin pattern. However, kelpfishes are more closely related to the hawkfishes and have a pointed snout and a jagged dorsal fin. These fish are found only in southern Australia, where they like to sit on rocks or among seaweeds and feed on small invertebrates.

Eastern Kelpfish *Chironemus marmoratus*

ID: 40cm. Mottled grey, brown or green with numerous white spots.

HABITAT/RANGE: Rocky reefs from southern Qld to eastern Vic.

NOTES: Groups are often found together in the surge zone.

HAWKFISHES (12 species)

Small colourful reef fish that like to perch on the bottom. They have a slightly elongated body, large highset eyes, spiny dorsal fins and pectoral fins with extended rays. Most species feed on invertebrates and small fishes, but a few consume plankton. Hawkfishes are found in pairs, or in a small group of females with one dominant male.

Spotted Hawkfish *Cirrhitichthys oxycephalus*

ID: 85cm. White with reddish-brown spots and blotches.

HABITAT/RANGE: Coral reefs from central WA to northern NSW.

NOTES: A protogynous hermaphrodite, with females able to change sex if they lose the dominant male.

WRASSES AND PARROTFISHES
(c.260 species)

Another large and complex family containing small and large fish that often look very different. Most have an elongated or slender body with a terminal mouth, prominent lips and a single dorsal fin. Nearly all wrasses have pretty colour patterns, that are often different for males, females and juveniles of the same species. Most are found in groups, with a dominant male and a harem of females. If the male dies the largest female changes sex and takes his place. Within the family are pigfish, tuskfish, Maori wrasse, fairy-wrasse, cleaner wrasse, flasher wrasse and razorfish, and recently the parrotfishes, cales and weed whiting, which used to be in their own family, were added. Wrasses eat invertebrates, small fish and zooplankton, and the parrotfishes eat algae and coral.

Eastern Blue Groper *Achoerodus viridis*

ID: 120cm. Male bright blue, female reddish brown.

HABITAT/RANGE: Rocky reefs from southern Qld. to eastern Vic.

NOTES: A cheeky fish that nudges divers to feed it sea urchins. Most popular dive sites in NSW have a resident population.

Female/juvenile.

Male

Coral Pigfish *Bodianus axillaris*

ID: 20cm. Male has reddish-brown head and body becoming white towards the tail. Female and juvenile black with large white spots.

HABITAT/RANGE: Coral reefs from central WA to northern NSW.

NOTES: Also known as hogfish, these wrasse pair up to mate and spawn.

Harlequin Tuskfish *Choerodon fasciatus*

ID: 30cm. Multicoloured fish with orange, green, blue and grey bands.

HABITAT/RANGE: Coral reefs from northern Qld to northern NSW.

NOTES: Tuskfish have protruding teeth and are generally seen alone or in small groups.

Western King Wrasse *Coris auricularis*

ID: 40cm. Male pink with a white band, female pink with a red stripe.

HABITAT/RANGE: Rocky reefs around the south-west corner of WA.

NOTES: Often seen in groups comprising a male and a group of females, foraging for food over sand or seaweed.

Western King Wrasse, male (above) and female.

Common Cleaner Wrasse *Labroides dimidiatus*

ID: 12cm. White and blue with a bold black stripe.

HABITAT/RANGE: Coral reefs from central WA to central NSW.

NOTES: Groups of these fish establish cleaning centres and clean other fish of parasites.

White-patch Razorfish *Iniistius aneitensis*

ID: 24cm. Cream colour with darker bands and a white blotch.

HABITAT/RANGE: Sandy bottoms on the Great Barrier Reef.

NOTES: Razorfish are very thin bodied and dive into the sand when threatened.

Rainbow Cale *Heteroscarus acroptilus*

ID: 24cm. Male yellow to green with black blotches and blue lines, female orange to brown.

HABITAT/RANGE: Weed-covered reefs from central NSW to southern WA.

NOTES: The colours of this species vary greatly to match the surrounding seaweeds.

Sharpnose Weed Whiting *Siphonognathus caninis*

ID: 10cm. Female reddish-brown to green with lighter blotchy stripe, male yellow to green with blue stripes.

HABITAT/RANGE: Weedy reefs from eastern Vic. to southern WA.

NOTES: Very elongated fish that hide in the weed and are not often seen.

Pacific Bullethead Parrotfish *Chlorurus spilurus*

ID: 37cm. Male bluish to brownish with purple and blue streaks on fins and face, female brown to maroon.

HABITAT/RANGE: Coral reefs off Qld and WA.

NOTES: Like most parrotfish this species hides under ledges at night and secrets a mucus cocoon around its body to protect it from predators.

GRUBFISHES (37 species)

Bottom-dwelling fish that grub in the sand for small crustaceans. These elongated fish have a flattened head, large eyes and a single dorsal fin. They are mostly observed sitting on their fins, and are found mostly in tropical waters.

Blacktail Grubfish *Parapercis queenslandica*

ID: 21cm. White with brown spots on body and black tail spot.

HABITAT/RANGE: Sandy bottoms from northern Qld to northern NSW.

NOTES: Grubfish are very curious of divers and if you want to get their attention simply dig in the sand with your fingers.

STARGAZERS (21 species)

Ambush predators that hide in the sand with only their eyes exposed, and snatch small fish and cephalopods. These strange fish have an elongated body, a large flat head, highset eyes and a wide upturned mouth. Many have venomous spines at the base of the pectoral fins, and some have lures in their mouth, a few species can also generate electric shocks.

Common Stargazer *Kathetostoma laeve*

ID: 75cm. Sandy colour with two large dark blotches.

HABITAT/RANGE: Sandy bottoms from central NSW to western SA.

NOTES: Many stargazers are only found in deep water, while this species is common in shallow water, but often hidden under a layer of sand.

THORNFISHES (2 species)

This small family of fish is only found in temperate waters. They have elongated bodies, large highset eyes, a narrow snout and two dorsal fins. Most have thorns on their gill covers. Bottom-dwellers, they hide between rocks and seaweed and feed on small crustaceans.

Thornfish *Bovichtus angustifrons*

ID: 30cm. Brown and cream blotched pattern with white spots on the head.

HABITAT/RANGE: Rocky reefs from southern NSW to western SA.

NOTES: This species is also called the Dragonet and is often seen under jetties in Port Phillip Bay.

BLENNIES (c.107 species)

A large and diverse family. These small fishes are elongated and slender with a blunt head, highset eyes, a single dorsal fin and slimy scaleless skin. Their teeth vary from comb-like to fangs, which is reflected in group names such as fang-blennies, combtooth blennies and sabretooth blennies. Blennies are bottom-dwelling fish that live in holes or under rocks and corals, and use these places to hide their eggs, which the male guards. They feed on algae, small invertebrates and zooplankton, depending on the species.

Eyelash Fang-Blenny *Meiacanthus atrodorsalis*

ID: 11cm. Pale blue and yellow with black stripe over eye.

HABITAT/RANGE: Coral reefs of the Great Barrier Reef.

NOTES: This species has large venomous teeth in its lower jaw for defence.

Tasmanian Blenny *Parablennius tasmanianus*

ID: 13cm. Pale brown to grey with darker blotches. Male has six bands.

HABITAT/RANGE: Shallow rocky reefs from southern NSW to western SA.

NOTES: Feeds on algae and hides in holes with only its head showing.

Smallspotted Combtooth Blenny.

Leopard Blenny *Exallias brevis*

ID: 14.5cm. White with orange or brown pattern of spots and bands.

HABITAT/RANGE: Coral reefs from central WA to northern NSW.

NOTES: A large blenny that likes to hide in branching hard corals.

Smallspotted Combtooth Blenny *Ecsenius stictus*

ID: 6cm. Pale brown with spots and dashes, a white lower head and black chin strap.

HABITAT/RANGE: Coral reefs off Qld.

NOTES: This species likes to perch on coral and feed on algae.

THREEFINS (44 species)

Small bottom-dwelling fish that feed on small invertebrates and are often overlooked. They look similar to blennies and gobies, having an elongated body and large highset eyes, but have a pointed snout, small scales and three separate dorsal fins. Some threefins have different colours between the sexes, with the males brightly coloured and the females drab.

Female.

Male.

Masked Threefin *Enneapterygius fuligicauda*

ID: 4cm. Male red with black head and tail, female mottled pinky-green.

HABITAT/RANGE: Coral reefs from northern Qld to central NSW.

NOTES: Quite secretive and are mostly seen sitting on the bottom keeping an eye out for prey and predators.

WEEDFISHES AND SNAKE BLENNIES
(>33 species)

Hiding among weeds and rocks, the weedfishes and snake blennies are not easy fish to see. Inhabiting temperate waters, currently 33 species are recognised in Australia, and several new species are awaiting description. Both have elongated bodies with a pointed snout and long dorsal fin. They differ with the weedfishes having large pectoral and ventral fins to perch on, while snake blennies have small fins and an eel-like body. These small fish eat small invertebrates and practise internal fertilisation, giving birth to live young.

Longnose Weedfish.

Longnose Weedfish *Heteroclinus tristis*

ID: 30cm. Yellow, red or brown with darker bands and spots.

HABITAT/RANGE: Weedy covered reefs off Vic, Tas and SA.

NOTES: Male and female look very similar, except the male has a higher first dorsal fin.

Dusky Snake Blenny *Ophiclinus antarcticus*

ID: 14cm. Colour varies from yellow to brown with mottled pattern.

HABITAT/RANGE: Rocky and weedy reefs of SA.

NOTES: A secretive fish that likes to hide under rocks and debris.

DRAGONETS (47 species)

Known to many Australians as stinkfish, because they lack scales and instead have mucus on their skin that smells. Dragonets are elongated fish with two dorsal fins, a small mouth and highset eyes. They walk or slide across the bottom looking for small invertebrates, spending most of their time on the bottom, except when spawning, when a pair will rise into the water column to release eggs and sperm.

Marble Dragonet *Synchiropus ocellatus*

ID: 8cm. Brown and cream blotched pattern.

HABITAT/RANGE: Coral and rocky reefs from northern Qld to central NSW.

NOTES: A small secretive fish that feeds mostly on copepods.

Painted Stinkfish *Synchiropus papilio*

ID: 13cm. Cream to brown with blotches. Male with additional blue patterns.

HABITAT/RANGE: Sandy bottoms from southern Qld to southern WA.

NOTES: A common species in temperate waters, often seen under jetties.

JAWFISHES (20 species)

Living in holes in the sand and rubble, all that is generally seen of a jawfish is its large head. These elongated fish have large eyes, a large mouth and a single long dorsal fin. They constantly maintain their home, spitting out sand that spills in. Jawfishes dart from their holes to eat plankton and small invertebrates. These fish are mouth brooders.

Halfnaked Jawfish *Opistognathus seminudus*

ID: 9cm. White with brown mottled pattern.

HABITAT/RANGE: Sandy bottoms on the Great Barrier Reef.

NOTES: A recently described species that is little known.

GOBIES (c.450 species)

A very large and complex family. These small fish have elongated
bodies, a round head, highset eyes and two dorsal fins. Most live
on the bottom in burrows, but others hide on corals and sponges.
Gobies have a varied diet, eating small invertebrates, fish and
particles found in the sand. Most lay eggs that are attached to
rocks or coral and guarded by the male. Within the family are
shrimpgobies, glidergobies, sandgobies, coral gobies, sponge
gobies and pygmy gobies.

Immaculate Glidergoby *Valenciennea immaculata*

ID: 13cm long, silvery-cream with two blue edged orange stripes.

HABITAT/RANGE: Sandy bottoms from central WA to central NSW.

NOTES: Seen in pairs grabbing mouthfuls of sand, which is filtered
for food particles.

Twin-spot Goby *Signigobius biocellatus*

ID: 10cm long, cream colour with brown blotches and two eye spots on the dorsal fins.

HABITAT/RANGE: Sand and rubble on the northern Great Barrier Reef.

NOTES: These gobies are always seen in pairs and move with a rocking motion when alarmed.

Blackchest Shrimpgoby *Amblyeleotris guttata*

ID: 11cm long. Cream colour with orange spots and black bars behind the head.

HABITAT/RANGE: Sandy bottoms from northern WA to southern Qld.

NOTES: Shrimpgobies live in a commensal relationship with pistol shrimps, sharing a burrow in the sand.

Decorated Sandgoby *Istigobius decorates*

ID: 13cm. Cream colour with darker spots and dashes.

HABITAT/RANGE: Sandy bottoms from northern WA to northern NSW.

NOTES: Sandgobies are generally seen on the sand under ledges.

DART GOBIES (25 species)

Look very similar to gobies, but most members of this family hover off the bottom and feed on zooplankton. These fish have elongated bodies, highset eyes and a projecting lower jaw. Within the family are the eel-like wormfish, the robust ribbongobies and the pretty firegobies.

Red Firegoby *Nemateleotris magnifica*

ID: 9cm. Yellow head, red and white body and a long dorsal fin.

HABITAT/RANGE: Sandy bottoms from NT to northern NSW.

NOTES: Seen in pairs, these fish dart into a burrow if alarmed.

SURGEONFISHES (56 species)

All possess very sharp spines or blades at the base of their tail for defence. These fish are oval shaped with a compressed body, a single dorsal fin, a small mouth and small scales. Most species have bright colours and many live in schools. Surgeonfishes graze on algae, with a few also eating plankton. There are a few different surgeonfish forms, including the tangs, bristletooth, unicornfish and sawtails.

Pencil Surgeonfish *Acanthurus dussumieri*

ID: 54cm. Pale blue to brown with yellow wavy lines and highlights. Juveniles are grey.

HABITAT/RANGE: Coral reefs from central WA to central NSW.

NOTES: Seen individually or in schools.

Blue Tang *Paracanthurus hepatus*

ID: 31cm. Bright blue with a black back and yellow and black tail.

HABITAT/RANGE: Coral reefs from northern Qld to central NSW.

NOTES: Usually live in small groups and hide in coral and under ledges when alarmed.

Paletail Unicornfish *Naso brevirostris*

ID: 60cm. Brown to grey with darker stripe pattern and a bony head spike.

HABITAT/RANGE: Coral reefs off WA and Qld.

NOTES: Juveniles of this species get washed south by currents and turn up on the south coast of NSW.

Australian Sawtail *Prionurus microlepidotus*

ID: 70cm. Grey colour with six bony plates with spines near tail.

HABITAT/RANGE: Coral and rocky reefs from central Qld to southern NSW.

NOTES: Seen in schools feeding on algae.

MOORISH IDOL (1 species)

The Moorish Idol looks like a bannerfish, but this striking fish is more closely related to the surgeonfish and is the only member of its family. This fish has a round compressed body, a long snout, a small mouth and a banner like dorsal fin. They are mostly seen in pairs, but do form into schools, and eat small invertebrates, sponges and coral polyps.

Moorish Idol *Zanclus cornutus*

ID: 23cm long, white and yellow with black bands.

HABITAT/RANGE: Coral reefs from central WA to northern NSW.

NOTES: These fish are pelagic spawners and have a long larval stage.

RABBITFISHES (16 species)

Found in tropical waters, rabbitfishes have an oval compressed body, a small mouth, a single dorsal fin and venomous fin spines. Some species school and other species are seen in pairs. They eat algae and seagrass, and are found on coral reefs, bays and in estuaries.

Goldlined Rabbitfish *Siganus lineatus*

ID: 43cm long, bluish-grey with yellow spots and stripes.

HABITAT/RANGE: Coral reefs from central WA to southern Qld.

NOTES: Care should always be taken around rabbitfish due to their venomous spines.

LEFT-EYED FLOUNDERS (52 species)

A very distinctive group of flattened fish that are split into three families based on several features, including the position of the eyes. The left-eyed flounders have their eyes on the left side, and like all flounders have an oval shaped compressed body. Mostly found in tropical waters, these bottom-dwelling fish like to hide in the sand and feed on small invertebrates and fish.

Panther Flounder *Bothus pantherinus*

ID: 30cm. Sandy-brown with lighter rings and spots.

HABITAT/RANGE: Sandy bottoms from central WA to southern NSW.

NOTES: Can change colour to blend into the bottom to catch prey or avoid predators.

RIGHT-EYED FLOUNDERS (6 species)

As the name suggests, the fish in this flounder family have their eyes on the right side of the body. All species live in temperate waters. These fish have close set eyes and asymmetrical pelvic fins. Right-eyed flounders mostly feed at night on small invertebrates and fishes. All flounders, and soles, start life with eyes on either side of the head, and as they grow one eye migrates until they both end up on the same side.

Greenback Flounder *Rhombosolea tapirina*

ID: 45cm. Green to brown with darker blotches.

HABITAT/RANGE: Sandy bottoms from southern NSW to western SA.

NOTES: Found from the shallows to depths of 100m.

SOLES (49 species)

Soles look very similar to flounders, but are generally smaller and slender with a pointed head and small mouth. Soles are also right eyed, have small fins and small eyes. These fish hide in the sand by day and feed at night on small fishes and invertebrates. Found in both tropical and temperate waters.

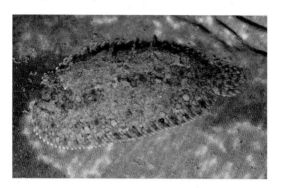

Southern Peacock Sole *Pardachirus hedleyi*

ID: 15cm. Light brown with light and dark blotches and rings.

HABITAT/RANGE: Sandy bottoms from central Qld. to southern NSW.

NOTES: Several soles have toxin glands at the base of their fins, including this species.

TRIGGERFISHES (24 species)

The triggerfishes, and their cousins the leatherjackets, share many similar features. They are oval shaped with a compressed body, have a small mouth, sandpaper-like skin instead of scales and a dorsal fin spine for defence, that can lock into position. The triggerfishes differ in having chisel-like teeth, the eyes positioned in front of the dorsal spine and the dorsal fin has three spines. These colourful tropical fish eat small invertebrates and algae, but a few species eat plankton. Triggerfishes can be territorial when guarding a nest of eggs.

Lagoon Triggerfish *Rhinecanthus aculeatus*

ID: 25cm. White with black patch and bars, also blue and yellow stripes.

HABITAT/RANGE: Lagoons and bays from central WA to central NSW.

NOTES: Like many triggerfish, this species has a hideout that it retreats to when alarmed.

LEATHERJACKETS AND FILEFISHES
(60 species)

The leatherjackets are well represented in Australia in both tropical and temperate waters. They vary greatly in body shape, most being oval, but others are elongated or circular. Leatherjackets have a single spine on the first dorsal fin, the eyes are located below this spine and their teeth are large. They eat small invertebrates, algae and even sea jellies. The smaller tropical species are known as filefish, with both sexes having similar colours. While the larger temperate species have different colours for the males and females.

Horseshoe Leatherjacket *Meuschenia hippocrepis*

ID: 60cm. Male blue and yellow, female light brown. Both have a horseshoe-shaped pattern on the side.

HABITAT/RANGE: Rocky reefs from eastern Vic. to southern WA.

NOTES: Most large leatherjackets are popular with anglers.

Harlequin Filefish *Oxymonacanthus longirostris*

ID: 12cm. Light blue with yellow spots.

HABITAT/RANGE: Coral reefs from central WA to northern NSW.

NOTES: These beautiful small fish are always seen in pairs and only eat Acropora coral polyps.

TEMPERATE BOXFISHES (8 species)

The boxfishes have a hard-shelled carapace encasing their body. These box-shaped fish are split into two families, with the temperate boxfishes having a rounded carapace and all the median fins protruding from a single opening. These fish have small fins, a small mouth and have different colours for males and females. These fishes are bottom feeders in temperate waters, blowing away sand to expose small invertebrates.

Male Ornate Cowfish.

Female.

Ornate Cowfish *Aracana ornata*

ID: 15cm. Male brown with blue and yellow patterns, female brown with cream-coloured stripes.

HABITAT/RANGE: Shallow reefs from eastern Vic. to western SA.

NOTES: These small fish have head and body horns, hence the name cowfish.

Male (top) and female Eastern Smooth Boxfish.

Eastern Smooth Boxfish *Anoplocapros inermis*

ID: 35cm. Yellow with brown spots. Mature males bluish.

HABITAT/RANGE: Rocky reefs from southern Qld to eastern Vic.

NOTES: Many boxfishes can secrete a toxic mucus, so should never be eaten or handled.

TROPICAL BOXFISHES (12 species)

Most species found in tropical waters, but a few range into temperate zones. These fish mostly have a square-shaped carapace, with individual holes for fins, mouth, gills and eyes. Within the family are also cowfish, with horns, and turretfish, which are triangular shaped. Some tropical boxfishes have the same colours for males and females, while others have different colours. They eat small invertebrates.

Thornback Cowfish *Lactoria fornasini*

ID: 23cm. Yellow to brown with blue spots and dashes.

HABITAT/RANGE: Bays and estuaries from central WA to central NSW.

NOTES: This species is usually solitary, only pairing up to mate.

Male (top) and female.

Black Boxfish *Ostracion meleagris*

ID: 25cm. Males blue and black with yellow and white spots, female black with white spots.

HABITAT/RANGE: Coral reefs from central WA to central NSW.

NOTES: These fish make a strange humming noise when mating.

PUFFERFISHES (63 species)

With the ability to inflate themselves to deter predators, the pufferfishes are well named. These fish also have poisonous skin and organs, and should never be eaten. The pufferfishes typically have a rounded body with prickly skin. They have a pointed snout with fused teeth and most eat algae or invertebrates. Pufferfish have bright colours, and the family varies considerably in size, with some over 1m long, and the small tobies and toadfish less than 15cm long. Found mostly in tropical waters.

Starry Puffer *Arothron stellatus*

ID: 100cm. Pale grey with black spots.

HABITAT/RANGE: Coral reefs from central WA to central NSW.

NOTES: Often seen resting on the bottom by day.

Weeping Toadfish *Torquigener pleurogramma*

ID: 21cm. White belly and brown back with white spots.

HABITAT/RANGE: Sandy bottoms from southern Qld. to central WA.

NOTES: This species likes to hide in the sand.

Honeycomb Toby *Canthigaster janthinoptera*

ID: 9cm. Brown with green and yellow spots.

HABITAT/RANGE: Coral reefs off WA and northern Qld. to northern NSW.

NOTES: Tobies are small, shy puffers that often hide under ledges.

PORCUPINEFISHES (12 species)

Closely related to the pufferfishes, they contain poisons and can inflate themselves. They differ in having longer spines covering their body and their teeth fused like a beak. Porcupinefish are generally found in tropical waters and feed at night on invertebrates. By day they rest on the bottom under ledges, coral or seaweed.

Blackblotched Porcupinefish *Diodon liturosus*

ID: 45cm. Brown with black blotches and yellow fins.

HABITAT/RANGE: Coral reefs from central WA to northern NSW.

NOTES: Feeds nocturnally on sea urchins and crustaceans.

SUNFISHES (5 species)

These are the heaviest of all the ray-finned bony fishes, with some weighing over 2,000kg. These strange oval-shaped fish look like they have been cut in half, as their tall dorsal and ventral fins sit far back on the body. Sunfishes have a hard body casing, a small mouth and fused teeth. These fish are ocean wanderers and feed on sea jellies and small invertebrates.

Bumphead Sunfish *Mola alexandrini*

ID: 300cm tall. Grey with white blotches.

HABITAT/RANGE: Open water around Australia.

NOTES: These massive fish sometimes come into shallow water to feed or get cleaned by other fish.

GLOSSARY

Barbel: Fleshy tentacle extension near the mouth.

Bioluminescent: Emission of light by living animals.

Cephalopod: Class of molluscs including the octopus, cuttlefish and squid.

Crustacean: Hard-shelled animals such as crabs, shrimps and lobsters.

Diurnal: Active by day.

Endemic: Restricted to a certain area, state or country.

Hermaphrodite: Animal having both female and male reproductive organs.

Invertebrate: Animals that lack a backbone.

Mimicry: Copying the features or colours of another animal.

Molluscs: Phylum of animals that typically have a foot and shell, like sea shells and snails.

Nocturnal: Active by night.

Ovate: Shaped like an egg.

Pelagic: Inhabiting open water.

Plankton: Small organisms, plant and animal, that drift with ocean currents.

Tunicate: Marine invertebrate group including sea squirts and salps.

Zooplankton: Small animal organisms that drift with ocean currents.

INDEX